Transforming Primary QTS

Primary Mathematics
across the Curriculum

Alice Hansen and Diane Vaukins

799319

First published in 2011 by Learning Matters Ltd

British Library Cataloguing in Publication Data
A CIP record for this book is available from the British Library

ISBN: 978 0 85725 605 8
This book is also available in the following e-book formats:
Adobe ebook ISBN: 978 0 85725 607 2
EPUB book ISBN: 978 0 85725 606 5
Kindle ISBN: 978 0 85725 608 9

Cover design by Toucan Design
Text design by Toucan Design
Project management by Deer Park Productions, Tavistock
Typeset by PDQ Typesetting Ltd, Newcastle-under-Lyme
Printed and bound in Great Britain by Bell & Bain Ltd, Glasgow

Learning Matters Ltd
20 Cathedral Yard
Exeter EX1 1HB
Tel: 01392 215560
info@learningmatters.co.uk
www.learningmatters.co.uk

MIX
Paper from
responsible sources
FSC® C007785

Contents

Introduction

This book is one of the first in the new Transforming Primary QTS series, which has been established to reflect current best practice and a more creative and integrated approach to the primary school curriculum. While mathematics is a subject that will keep a strong and discrete identity through current curriculum review, there is a clear movement within schools to approach mathematics teaching and learning in ways that engage and inspire children.

This book encourages you as a trainee teacher to take a critical and creative look at how you can make best use of mathematics to support learning across the curriculum.

The importance of mathematics should not be underestimated. Not only is it a core National Curriculum subject in its own right, it also provides children with the skills of reasoning, problem-solving and communication that can be used as tools to learn all subjects.

About the book

This book takes a practical look at how you can develop children's mathematical knowledge, skills and understanding by offering a number of opportunities to address many of the challenges of learning and teaching mathematics in a cross-curricular way.

The book is presented in two parts. Part 1 focuses on the content of the mathematics curriculum and how each programme of study can be taught through other curriculum subjects or used and applied in order to teach other subjects. You are encouraged to take a wide-ranging approach to identify opportunities for developing children's mathematics attainment.

Part 2 takes a look at some of the wider issues of using mathematics in your professional role in primary education, including essential guidance on current debates and practice. You will be guided through the intricacies of using mathematics to:

- organise learning environments, education visits, timetables, planning and budgeting;
- use data to improve your teaching and children's learning and progress;
- carry out practitioner research as a form of professional development.

Learning Matters have published a number of other mathematics-related titles. This book is complementary to these because it moves on from the core knowledge and understanding required to teach mathematics effectively. At times you will be directed to these in this book.

Using this book

Throughout this book the authors have drawn upon their extensive experience of teaching and mentoring trainee teachers to present a wide range of case studies that you can adapt and use in your own classroom. The activities provided in each chapter will help you become actively engaged in strengthening your subject knowledge and developing your skills in teaching mathematics. Each chapter concludes with a review of learning, and poses questions related to the content for you to reflect upon. Suggested responses to these self-assessment questions are included at the end of the book.

Mathematics across the curriculum

To help you find your way around this book, you can use the following tables to locate where particular subjects and themes are discussed.

Table 1 shows where National Curriculum subjects are referred to.

Subject	Chapter	Brief description
English	1	Using graphical representation to support persuasive writing
	1, 4	Using reasoning to sequence events and develop a clear structure
	2, 3	Using language for effective communication
	2, 3	Using story to develop mathematical concepts
	4	Using ordinal language to sequence events
Science	4	Understanding units of measure
	4	Using data to make predictions
	5	Living things: observing birds at the feeding station
	5	Using Carroll diagrams to present findings about floating and sinking
Design and technology	1	A mentor reminds a trainee teacher about making links between a mathematics lesson on transformation and a DT lesson later that day
	3	Planning a garden to scale
	3	Creating dwellings with 3D solids
	4	Designing and making Greek sandals
ICT	1	Using reasoning and data to share and exchange ideas
	2	Retrieving stored information and working with a range of data to think about ways it can be presented
	4	Creating flow diagrams
	4	Sharing and exchanging information (blogging)
	4	How ICT can improve the efficiency and accuracy of solving problems
	5	Analysing data using ICT
History	2, 4	Using number to develop chronological understanding and historical enquiry
	4	The Babylonians
	5	Using archival materials to study Victorian Blackpool

Geography	1	Presenting data found about a location
	2	Using mathematics trails to understand children's locality
	3	Using items to describe what places are like
	3	Using co-ordinates to describe where places are
	4	Temperature of hot climates
	4	Recycling and sustainable development
	4	Designing a weather station
	4	Maps, coordinates
	5	Direction and scale
	5	Weather
Art and design	2	Reproducing hieroglyphs
	4	Using materials
Music	2	Exploring the links between music and pattern
	4	Notation and timing
Physical education	2	Exploring pattern and number through dance
	4	Using time to assess running speed
	6	Setting out a rounders pitch
	6	Organising sports days
Personal, social and health education and citizenship	5	Healthy eating and working collaboratively
	7	The self-esteem of children
Modern foreign languages	2	Cultural differences in the way numbers are presented
	4	Learning about measurement using a Content and Languages Integrated Learning (CLIL) approach

Table 1 Cross-curricular links

Other issues and themes are also dealt with, and these are shown in Table 2.

3

Issue	Chapter	Brief description
Learning outside of the classroom	2	Mathematical trails
	6	Planning an educational visit
Promoting home–school links	7	Reporting to parents
Health and safety	6	Planning an educational visit
Classroom organisation	6	Designing the classroom
	6	Managing resources
Teacher CPD	8	Using the 'improving learning and teaching process' as CPD
	8	Using research and literature to improve learning and teaching
Assessment	1	Using evidence in other curriculum subjects to complete APP using and applying grids
	7	Using APP
	7	Collecting data
	7	A critical look at SATs
	7	RAISEonline
Multicultural	3	Using tangrams to explore congruency, similarity, area, perimeter and shape
Timetabling	6	Guidance surrounding hours to be spent teaching curriculum subjects

Table 2 Other issues

PART 1
THE MATHEMATICS CURRICULUM

1. Mathematics as a core skill

Learning Outcomes

This chapter explores:
- how mathematics is used in the world around us;
- how we should make links between mathematics and all national curriculum subjects;
- issues relating to planning and assessment;
- the core skills related to using and applying; these are reasoning, problem-solving and communication.

Professional Standards for QTS

Q3 (a) Be aware of the professional duties of teachers and the statutory framework within which they work.

Q8 Have a creative and constructively critical approach towards innovation, being prepared to adapt their practice where benefits and improvements are identified.

Q14 Have a secure knowledge and understanding of their subjects/curriculum areas and related pedagogy to enable them to teach effectively across the age and ability range for which they are trained.

Q15 Know and understand the relevant statutory and non-statutory curricula and frameworks, including those provided through the National Strategies, for their subjects/curriculum areas, and other relevant initiatives applicable to the age and ability range for which they are trained.

Q17 Know how to use skills in literacy, numeracy and ICT to support their teaching and wider professional activities.

Q23 Design opportunities for learners to develop their literacy, numeracy and ICT skills.

Q25 (b) Build on prior knowledge, develop concepts and processes, enable learners to apply new knowledge, understanding and skills and meet learning objectives.

Using mathematics in the world around us

Many adults and children hold the perception that mathematics is often something that is 'done', rather than something that is used every day as part of our lives and are often unaware of how they use mathematical skills in their everyday tasks.

Activity

To help you think about mathematics as a core skill, below is a list of tasks that you may find yourself undertaking. Choose one or two and identify what mathematical skills you need in order to achieve the desired outcome.

Setting an alarm to wake up at 7:30 a.m.	Working out what time to leave home to arrive at your placement school	Checking the water temperature in the shower	Working out what to buy at the shop when you have £5 only
Deciding what to wear	Gathering equipment for an art lesson	Planning and preparing for a summer break	Decorating your bedroom
Negotiating rotas in student accommodation	How to dry the washing	Having friends for a meal	Posting a card in time to reach a friend on his/her birthday

The activity above was designed to encourage you to consider how everyday tasks require a number of mathematical skills. For example, a deceptively simple task in deciding what to wear will include:

- identifying the current and forecast weather (temperature, wet/dry, sunny/cloudy);
- considering the day's activity (is it fit for purpose: work, pleasure, method of travel);
- the length of your activity/day (the passing of time and telling time);
- choice from the available wardrobe (combinations);
- aesthetic considerations (does it look appealing, pattern, colour).

How did you get on with the task? If you found it difficult to think about the numerous skills that were used and applied in the tasks above, perhaps this helps you to realise that you could be one of the many people who do not relate mathematics to the everyday tasks that you carry out.

It could be argued that you are able to function and carry out these tasks without the mathematical knowledge underpinning the activity. However, teachers are required to assess children's mathematical ability across the curriculum and not only within a mathematics lesson. Therefore, unless you are able to identify mathematics within everyday activities, your planning, teaching and assessment are likely to be very narrow in their approach to mathematics. Indeed, you may overlook evidence of a child's mathematical attainment in other parts of the school day.

Recognising and appreciating mathematics

Recognising mathematics in all subjects

Read the following case study and consider what learning opportunities the children were missing out on because of the way that Tamsin approached the two lessons in a discrete (unconnected) manner.

Case Study: Making links between lessons

Tamsin is a trainee teacher working with a Year 5/6 class. She is following the teacher's medium-term planning for the four-week duration of her placement.

In the morning Tamsin teaches a mathematics transformation lesson focusing on translation, reflection and rotation. Later that day, she is observed teaching a design and technology lesson where the children analyse wallpaper samples and discuss how the pattern was created.

During feedback, her mentor, Phil, comments on how he was surprised Tamsin did not model any mathematical language related to transformation. He also notes that only a small group of children were able to refer to the work they had been doing in their mathematics lesson during their afternoon work.

After some discussion it becomes apparent to both Phil and Tamsin that she did not make the connection between the two lessons herself. They talk about how she will address this in the future through careful planning and improved subject knowledge, as well as how an important aspect of her role is to model mathematical language across all subjects.

In order to address today's revelation, she decides that the children will be involved in making a display of their own wallpaper creations showing the mathematics they used in order to create the design.

Links to the National Curriculum

The mathematics objectives that Tamsin had in mind during her unit of work were that the children would be able to *visualise and describe movements using appropriate language* (Ma3, 3a) and *transform objects in practical situations ... visualise and predict the position of a shape following a rotation, reflection or translation* (Ma3, 3b). In design and technology the children were developing, planning and communicating ideas, specifically developing ideas and explaining them clearly (D&T 1b), planning (D&T 1c), and communicating design ideas in different ways (D&T 1d).

What Tamsin had omitted to see was that the children should have been using appropriate vocabulary in both lessons. The key skills (DfE, 1999, page 20) are embedded throughout the programmes of study in the National Curriculum. The key skills particularly practised in this case study should have been communication and problem-solving. Furthermore, the *thinking skill* (page 22) (helping with the 'knowing how' rather than simply the 'knowing what') that should have been most prominent in this case study is reasoning. Crucially, the children *using precise language to explain what they are thinking* (page 22) during communication will support effective reasoning. This will be discussed in more depth later in this chapter.

Activity

In light of the case study and the introduction of this chapter, why was it important that Tamsin should be able to recognise the connection between her mathematics and design and technology lessons?

Why is it important for all teachers to be able to recognise mathematics in all subjects and parts of the school day?

It is essential that you are able to recognise when mathematics is being used as a tool to learn other curriculum subjects. The above case study and explanation of National Curriculum links demonstrates how Tamsin's teaching would have more effectively supported the children's learning if she had seen the links between the morning's mathematics lesson and the content of the design and technology lesson in the afternoon.

External drivers for appreciating mathematical links

Planning and timetabling
By carefully planning learning experiences that are explicitly linked, it is possible to:

- cover a substantial number of curriculum objectives in a shorter period of time;
- make explicit the links across the artificial subject divisions that the curriculum creates;
- encourage children to use and apply mathematical skills in a range of meaningful contexts;
- approach tasks flexibly using a mathematician's disposition.

You can read more about the pedagogical reasons for cross-curricular approaches to teaching as well as how timetable constraints also often pragmatically require integrated approaches to learning in Chapter 6, but ultimately, it should be every teacher's aim for children to recognise and appreciate mathematics in the world around us.

As you are a trainee teacher, you may sometimes find difficulty in making links, as Tamsin did in the case study. Without being involved in the longer-term planning, what is obvious during curriculum development may not be so clear to you as a trainee teacher working from and adapting already established plans. This is specifically why you are encouraged to 'make planning your own' and discuss ideas with your mentor in school.

Activity

When you are next on placement, talk to your class teacher, mentor, the mathematics subject leader or mathematics specialist teacher about how they plan for cross-curricular links between mathematics and other subjects.

If possible, ask to see how their planning in the longer term develops, and discuss with them the process that their planning follows to consider cross-curricular links.

Assessing mathematics

In addition to using cross-curricular teaching methods to respond to planning and timetabling constraints, it is also possible to draw on evidence from a wider range of sources in order to assess children's mathematical attainment. The case study below demonstrates how a trainee teacher was encouraged to use Assessing Pupil Progress (APP) mathematics grids to assess a focus child's progress, and think about drawing on the wider evidence they had to make decisions about the child's level of attainment.

To access the full APP grids for mathematics, go to **http://nationalstrategies.standards.dcsf. gov.uk/node/47548**. The guidelines specifically related to the case study below can be found at **http://nationalstrategies.standards.dcsf.gov.uk/node/64668**.

Case Study: Using assessment evidence from beyond the mathematics lesson

The following transcript is taken from a mentor/trainee discussion about how the trainee, Gurjit, is getting on with his set placement task about using Assessing Pupil Progress (APP) grids in mathematics. Pauline, his mentor, is helping Gurjit to consider evidence beyond that collected during mathematics lessons. Gurjit is placed in a Year 2 class and they are discussing Harry's attainment.

Pauline: So tell me how you are getting on with Harry's attainment record.

Gurjit: I have had a go now at completing the maths APP grid, thinking about the lessons that you and I have taught since I arrived.

Pauline: Great. Of course as we discussed last time, it is important to remember that you won't see evidence pertaining to all the bullets in the grid over your six-week placement because the APP grids should be used over a longer period.

$\longrightarrow$

Gurjit: Yes.

Pauline: So let's have a look at what you have here. Oh, I see that you have not been able to highlight anything about problem-solving?

Gurjit: That's right. I have realised that I haven't planned for a lot of problem-solving in my lessons yet. I also have realised that I have not really been focusing on Ma1 – using and applying – at all in my lessons. That is so embarrassing!

Pauline: OK, it is good that you have picked that up, and you have actually come to a realisation that a lot of teachers in school also came to when they started using APP. It isn't that we 'teach to the grid' but the grids are helping us to find the gaps in our own teaching and the process is helping us to see where we can improve our own work. Good. I do have to say that I'm surprised you haven't identified where Harry might be in terms of problem-solving and communicating though.

Gurjit: Well, he is a high level 2 in the other areas of maths, but I can't just put that down for using and applying too!

Pauline: Spot on, Gurjit. But, although you haven't particularly focused on these areas in maths, what have you been doing with the children in persuasive writing at the moment?

Gurjit: We've been writing to the council about the proposed new playground.

Pauline: And?

Gurjit: I've been encouraging the children to include graphs and tables to help their argument! Oh yes, I see that now! The guidance here says *identifying key facts/relevant information ... use diagrams ... move between different representations of a problem, e.g. a situation described in words, a diagram, etc.* Oh my goodness, Harry could do that with little help from me.

Pauline: Yes, it seems that Harry has demonstrated that he was operating at level 2 in problem-solving during your English unit last week. Absolutely. Let's look at level 3 then. *Select the mathematics they use in a wider range of classroom activities.* Hmmm. Did you tell Harry to use the tables and charts that he used, or did he select which ones were most appropriate?

Gurjit: Oh, I think I did. Sorry.

Pauline: That's ok, Gurjit. Don't apologise. Instead, how could you celebrate with Harry about how he used maths effectively in his persuasive writing, and then talk with him about how he can select his own representations next time?

$\rightarrow$

Gurjit: That's straightforward. We're moving on to designing holiday brochures in English to continue our work on persuasive writing, but it also ties in nicely to our geography work. I could encourage him to think about the best ways to present some of the data they have found out about their location.

Pauline: Sounds good.

Gurjit: I could also show him a range of other tourist brochures and catalogues to show him how companies really use those sorts of details to inform their clients. Oh, this will be great!

Pauline: I'm so pleased to see your enthusiasm about linking English and geography in this way, and also that you have seen how maths can also be used here too. So Gurjit, to conclude, what is one thing that you will be taking from this part of our tutorial today?

Gurjit: Well, I have two actually. I have to reappraise my assessments to see if there is any evidence from outside the actual maths lessons that I can use to identify the children's attainment level. I also have to think some more about how maths can be used to communicate and solve problems. The children were using the diagrams, tables and graphs all last week and I never once referred to it as maths skills, because we were in English lessons! I'm going to change that straight away, especially because they were all so motivated by the persuasive writing unit and so they should see how maths helps to persuade too.

Chapter 7 further discusses the role of assessment and how you will be expected to use assessment data to improve your teaching and also children's learning across the curriculum. However, this chapter uses the case study above to illustrate how you should be aware of children's mathematical understanding throughout the school day and not simply during more formal mathematics lessons.

Links to the National Curriculum

Although the case study above focused on the using and applying mathematics APP grids, it is possible for you to see that mathematics was used to support writing, covering English objectives: *Use clear structure to organise their writing and vary their writing to suit the purpose and reader* (En31d and e). Furthermore, by creating a context related to their geography work they were able to make observations about where things are located (POS 4a) and recognise how the environment may be improved and sustained (POS 5b). The children were also revising the geography objectives through this work. Engagement with the keys skills of application of number, working with others, and problem-solving (page 21) was also possible. The main thinking skills involved in this case study were information processing, reasoning and enquiry skills (page 22).

The next section will look at using and applying mathematics by exploring the importance of being able to recognise mathematics in all subjects and parts of the school day. It will also help you to draw out mathematical experiences in children's learning for them to be able to recognise and appreciate mathematics.

Using and applying mathematics within and beyond the curriculum

We identified above how mathematics underpins many actions in our everyday lives. In Chapters 2–5 we will explore how the mathematical skills and processes (known as *use and application* in the National Curriculum) should be interwoven with mathematical (and other) content. However, the remainder of this chapter intentionally offers a lens on mathematical use and application and how this pervades all areas of the curriculum. It is essential to do this in order to demonstrate the importance of these skills. In doing so, this section sets out a framework for the remaining chapters in Part 1 of this book.

Much research has identified the lack of using and applying seen in primary schools. For example, the Ofsted (2008) report, *Understanding the score* identified that children often lack opportunities to use and apply mathematics and to see connections between aspects of mathematics. Additionally, the Williams Review identified that:

> *Two issues only are singled out: the need for an increased focus on the 'use and application' of mathematics and on the vitally important question of the classroom discussion of mathematics. It is often suggested that 'mathematics itself is a language' but it must not be overlooked that only by constructive dialogue in the medium of the English language in the classroom can logic and reasoning be fully developed – the factors at the very heart of embedded learning in mathematics.*

(Williams, 2008, page 4)

Both of these reports are discussed in more detail in Chapter 8. However, what is important to be aware of at this stage is that 'using and applying' involves three key underpinning skills, which will be discussed and defined here. These are reasoning, problem-solving and communication (DfES, 2000). It is important to remember that the three skills are interwoven. Although these are broken down for the discussion that follows, the three aspects interact with each other and are not mutually exclusive. Above, Williams provides an example for us where communication is crucial for reasoning. Furthermore, the three interwoven aspects enable children to reflect upon and discuss their work and its quality, and develop their understanding about what they can do to improve it. This in turn raises their attainment (Jenkins and Lyle, 2010; Topping *et al.*, 2003).

Reasoning

Reasoning has always been, and remains, a crucial aspect of mathematical development (DfEE, 1999; Hanna, 2000; NCTM, 2000; Nunes *et al.*, 2007; Stylianides, 2007). However, the term 'reasoning' is often used among mathematics educators without defining it because there is an implicit assumption that there is a universal agreement on its meaning (Yackel and Hanna, 2003).

Research Focus

Until recently, most educationalists defined reasoning narrowly. For example, the behaviourist Thorndike (1922) explained reasoning as an organised hierarchy of connections with habits already acquired to solve novel problems. Others, including Piagetians, interpreted reasoning simply as logic (see Inhelder and Piaget, 1958, page 305). One notable exception to this was the late nineteenth-century mathematics educator Pierce, who identified that reasoning abilities were required for mathematical inquiry (Campos, 2010). However, more recently mathematics educators' definitions of reasoning have broadened significantly. For example, *reasoning helps children to create, deduce, apply, explore, predict, hypothesise and test* (National Strategies, 2010, online).

The purpose of reasoning

We believe that although reasoning still involves understanding the rules of logic, it does so much more than this. Reasoning helps children to make sense and keep track of their own and others' thinking, which in turn supports the sharing and evaluation of each other's approaches. It enables children to discuss and record their thinking (including explanations and choices using correct mathematical vocabulary). Reasoning helps children to identify and explore patterns, properties and relationships, therefore understanding the mathematical structures upon which more complex ideas are formed. In turn, knowledge about these structures enables children to make deductions and collect further evidence. Finally, reasoning enables children to effectively choose and use the most appropriate resources to think mathematically which in turn offers an opportunity to refine their thinking, another mathematical skill.

Reasoning involves:

- classification;
- deduction;
- explanation;
- finding patterns;
- inferring;
- logic;
- making connections;

- mapping;
- organising information;
- proof;
- reflection;
- sorting;
- trial and error.

Research Focus: Developing reasoning skills

Research demonstrates that one of the significant causes of underachievement in mathematics is that children rely on rote learning and superficial reasoning (e.g. Heibert, 2003; Palm, 2008).

This is reflected in Boesen et al.'s (2010) research. They analysed the mathematical reasoning used by children in a Swedish national test. They found that when children were confronted with a question that they had encountered in their textbooks, they solved it using rote methods. In these tasks, the children were not required to use or demonstrate understanding of the mathematical content or the method they used and relied on what Bergqvist (2007) calls *imitative reasoning*.

However, when the children were presented with non-typical questions, those who were most successful had used creative mathematically founded reasoning (CMR) that required both creativity and understanding. Boesen et al. define CMR as requiring three conditions.

1. **Novelty**. A new (to the reasoner) sequence of solution reasoning is created, or a forgotten sequence is recreated.

2. **Plausibility**. There are arguments supporting the strategy choice and/or strategy implementation, motivating why the conclusions are true or plausible.

3. **Mathematical foundation**. The arguments are anchored in intrinsic mathematical properties of the components involved in the reasoning.

(Boesen et al., 2010, page 94)

Sarama and Clements (2009a, page 337) may offer help for teachers in developing reasoning skills. They identify how educational experiences can help children to learn reasoning skills that they can use through their life. They suggest that using many examples that may appear different in surface structure, but have the same underlying structure, may be an effective way to develop reasoning abilities in children. This is in contrast to the popular view that children should receive examples that are varied in content and structure.

You can read the Chapter 6 case study 'Planning the sports day' to see an example of a trainee using the same underlying structure in two tasks.

The following case study exemplifies how a class of Year 4/5 children used reasoning in a task they were presented with by their trainee teacher, Lizzy. Can you tell what 'subject' lesson Lizzy is teaching?

Case Study: Setting up a 'mission to Mars'

Lizzy begins the first lesson of the day by showing the class a television news clip (**www.dailymail.co.uk/sciencetech/article-1349342/The-REAL-Big-Brother-Mock-mission-Mars-ready-land-red-planet-233-days-520-day-simulation.html**) about a Russian-based space crew who were simulating a mission to Mars that is taking them 520 days to carry out.

She then provides for them a sheet titled 'What do astronauts eat in space?', which includes information about astronauts eating three meals a day plus snacks, just as they would when they are on Earth. It goes on to explain the types of food available. They learn that tortillas are often used instead of bread so fewer crumbs are made (which could fly around the spacecraft and damage machinery). They also find out that salt and pepper don't look like they do on Earth, because they have to be suspended in liquid so that they don't float away. Finally, they learn that astronauts are able to select their own menus for the duration of the journey well in advance of leaving home, and that the order in which the astronauts were planning to eat them were important as they can't be changed on the spacecraft (Watson, 2008).

Lizzy then provides the children with a second sheet titled 'Keeping it clean', which explains how astronauts change their shirts, socks and underwear every two days, and their trousers once a week. There is no opportunity to wash clothes, so once worn they are disposed of. The processes of showering and housework are also explored.

The children are very enthusiastic about the notion of living in space. Lizzy explains to them that she thought that it would be interesting to see how much food and clothing would be required for the astronauts on the mock mission to Mars. The children agree and so the investigation for the morning begins. The children decide what they can find out from the information given. They decide that they can work in groups to identify:

- the number of meals and snacks required for each astronaut (and therefore the whole crew) over the 520 days;
- what space would be required to (a) store the food and (b) hold the disposed-of, crushed packaging;

$\rightarrow$

- how many clothes would be required;
- what space would be required to store the clothes a) prior to wearing and b) after wearing.

They also agree that they will send their findings to the Institute for Medical and Biological Problems in Moscow, the location of the experiment, once they have written it up.

Links to the National Curriculum

Teaching in this way, Lizzy has been able to integrate many National Curriculum subjects in an innovative way to engage the children thoroughly in their learning. To achieve the final outcome, many subjects and key skills will have been studied or used at some point: geography, science, thinking skills and problem-solving as well as the Healthy Schools initiative.

However, the main areas of study are connected to the final questions that the children decided to answer as well as the method of sending their findings to the Institute for Medical and Biological Problems. This would mainly involve ICT, mathematics and English, specifically the following.

English:
- Sequence events and recount them in appropriate detail (En3 1a).
- Use a clear structure to organise their writing (En3 1d).
- Vary their writing to suit the purpose and reader (En3 1e).
- Assemble and develop ideas on paper and on screen (En3 2b).

ICT:
- How to share and exchange information in a variety of forms, including email (3a).
- To be sensitive to the needs of the audience and think carefully about the content and quality when communicating information (3b).

Maths:
- Choose and use an appropriate way to calculate and explain their methods and reasoning (Ma 2 4d).
- Break down a more complex problem or calculation into simpler steps before attempting a solution; identify the information needed to carry out tasks (Ma2 1b).
- Organise work and refine ways of recording (Ma2 1f).

Problem-solving

All humans are naturally problem-solvers who use incubation, insight and creativity (Hélie and Sun, 2010). We suggest that this innate ability is what has developed humankind through time. As a trainee teacher you must acquire the skills to become a very competent problem-solver in the classroom as you juggle many competing demands and have to make efficient and effective decisions. Just as your role requires good problem-solving skills, it is likely that the future work of the children you teach will require them to be efficient and effective problem-solvers themselves.

Williams (2008) explains that children have to be given the time and space to tackle problems in mathematics lessons if they are to be confident and competent problem-solvers. You might be asking yourself if problem-solving is innate, why does it need to be taught, and why does problem-solving require such time to be dedicated to it?

The purpose of problem-solving

In his book *What is the point of school?*, Guy Claxton (2008, page 30) writes that *education professionals do foresee a range of problems and societal changes that will contribute to the development of an unstable and disconcerting world.*

He goes on to present the basis of a curriculum that would help children to *thrive in such a complicated and uncertain world.* These include:

- human rights;
- statistics and probability;
- empathy;
- managing risk;
- negotiation/mediation;
- ecology;
- how to think;
- epistemology;

- collaboration;
- literacy;
- global awareness;
- imagination;
- ethics;
- healthy scepticism;
- body awareness;
- neuroscience;

- resilience;
- creativity;
- will-power;
- giving and taking feedback;
- relaxation.

He explains *the most striking thing about this list is that many of the items are not 'subjects' at all as we currently recognise them, but qualities, traits, values and habits of mind. And there is nothing at all on the list that represents a body of knowledge that can simply be mastered* (Claxton, 2008, pages 30–31). We see that this not only provides a purpose for problem-solving in school, but offers us a broad context and definition of problem-solving.

A problem with 'real-life' problems

A 'real' problem is not necessarily one that relates to real life. We find ourselves disheartened when we see trainee teachers finding tenuous links to real life because they think that they are required to inject meaningfulness into a task. Furthermore, be careful not to make assumptions about what you may consider is 'real' to the children you teach. For example, not all the children you teach may have a television or receive pocket money. Therefore, ensure you get to know each child in your placement classroom as well as you can, before setting problems that you assume are 'real' for them. When planning, it is important to heed Bishop's (2001, page 102) findings. He warns that developing learning contexts and investigations demand

> attention on the part of the teacher to focus the pupils' attention on mathematical values, and it requires appreciation of the asymmetrical aspect of the teaching process to ensure that the pupils don't just assimilate the teacher's personal view ... [so] ... if you are teaching a class of students where some of them have a very different cultural background to the mainstream culture, be very sensitive and careful about your values teaching.

A simple internet search for 'real life maths problems' brought up a site where teachers could post lesson plans and resources to help each other. The first resource we clicked on provided a PowerPoint file that is used as the basis for the activity below.

Activity

Part A

The first PowerPoint slide contained a question similar to the following.

> There are 137 newspapers and 64 magazines in the paper boy's bag. How many items will he have to carry altogether?

It went on to require the children to highlight the key words and to choose the correct operation. It then demonstrated the calculation as the teacher expected the children to record it.

Reflect on the resource slide above. Identify as many issues as you can, related to problem-solving, using and applying mathematics and teaching and learning more generally.

Part B

After several similar slides the teacher was using for demonstration purposes, the final slide presents questions posed that are very similar to those below.

When you are reading through them, think particularly about the implications of these happening for real.

1. Our library has 987 books it in. 572 are burned in a fire. How many have we got left?
2. There are 385 marbles in George's tin and Sam has 639 marbles. How many marbles are there altogether?
3. Mr Jones is feeling particularly greedy and so eats 437 sweets on Wednesday. Then he eats 607 on Thursday. How many sweets has he eaten in total?

4. The farmer has relocated 528 haystacks so far but he needs to relocate 962 haystacks in total. How many haystacks does he have left to move?

5. Now write some of your own word problems. Solve them, showing your working out.

The first slide in the activity may reveal a lot about the teacher's knowledge and understanding of mathematics, and also his/her confidence in teaching mathematics. Which of the following issues did you recognise? Did you identify others?

- The problem is not particularly realistic – the child could not realistically carry these items altogether.

- The teacher requires the children to follow a particular method of recording (which may not be an issue if the children require further practice on it, but it is unlikely that this is an appropriate method of recording for all the children in the class).

- The objective for the lesson is not clear. Is it for children to be able to identify what the most important pieces of information are in the word problem; is it to be able to use and apply mathematics in a real-life context; is it to carry out a particular calculation method, or perhaps a combination of these?

- The question uses the stereotype of 'paper boy'.

Furthermore, the teacher does not appear to be developing a class ethos where discussion and finding things out are encouraged. Vygotsky (1987, page 150) reminds us that *direct teaching on concepts is impossible and fruitless. A teacher who tries to do this usually accomplishes nothing but empty verbalism, a parrot-like repetition of words by the child, simulating a knowledge of the corresponding concepts but actually covering up a vacuum.*

What did you make of the four questions? Some issues could include the following.

1. Children may become upset at the thought of the library being on fire.

2. The jars would need to be very large and would be too heavy for the boys to hold that many marbles.

3. Mr Jones (the teacher), presumably, could not (and should not!) eat that many sweets.

4. Haystacks may not be familiar to the children. One farmer is unlikely to have that many haystacks on his farm.

There are other issues such as the expectation that the children make up equally ridiculous problems for each other to solve. This does not particularly help the children to see appropriate use and application of mathematics. More importantly, another issue exists for children being able to access the problems because of their reading ability. This latter issue is explored further in Chapter 7.

The Primary Strategy and Ofsted tend to use problem-solving very narrowly, to include word problems that are solved through simple one- or two-step calculation (see DfES, 2003; HMI,

2002). There is a wide literature base that identifies how *conventional mathematics word problems are not aligned with the typical learning goals and expectations* (Green and Emerson, 2010, page 113).

Research Focus: Authentic tasks

Kramarski and Revach (2009) explain how mathematical problem-solving should use authentic tasks. They explain how authentic problem-solving requires understanding of the three mathematical skill areas:

- reproduction skills (application of routine algorithms and technical skills);
- connection skills (identifying and interpreting problem-solving skills and mathematical knowledge);
- reflection skills (having insight about the processes needed to solve a problem).

Kramarski and Revach (2009) identify that planning and implementing authentic tasks foster children's learning. Teachers require higher-order thinking skills and appropriate pedagogical knowledge in order to be able to plan tasks of this nature.

What does problem-solving involve?

We prefer to think of problem-solving in its widest sense, as purposeful and real or engaging tasks that require children to use:

- connections;
- discussion;
- enquiry (planning, deciding, organising, interpreting, reasoning and justifying);
- imagination, inventiveness and diverse strategies;
- investigation;
- justification;
- persistence (what Sarama and Clements, 2009b, call a *willingness to experiment*);
- representations to support the process;
- trial and error.

This definition enables us to use mathematical problem-solving as a skill throughout the curriculum and not just limited to word problems in mathematics lessons.

Activity

Think about some mathematics teaching you have undertaken that you considered effective. Note down why it was successful. Now think about the extent to which you encouraged the children to utilise the elements of problem-solving listed above. You may also find the following questions helpful.

To what extent:
1. Did you explicitly plan for problem-solving opportunities?
2. Did you actively encourage children to use problem solving strategies, including
   (a) posing questions;
   (b) sharing and discussing their ideas;
   (c) using a range of recording methods?
3. Did you formatively assess the children's problem-solving attainment, and later plan to develop it?
4. Was the mathematics meaningful to the children?

Now that you have had an opportunity to reflect on your teaching specifically in relation to problem-solving, talk with a colleague about how you may have taught this differently.

Communication

Communication can be broadly conceived in two ways: written communication and verbal communication. Each of these is discussed below and while they are treated separately here in order to discuss them, in the classroom the two aspects will be intertwined.

Activity
Think about all the ways that you communicate and list the purpose for those methods.
Answer the following questions, keeping in mind your methods of communication and the purpose for them.
- Do you ever write for yourself only, or for a small target audience?
- Do you prefer to write your ideas down, or talk about them?
- What is the main purpose of your writing emails, texts, academic assignments, letters, poetry, or ...?
- How often is your writing temporary (for example shopping lists)?
- How often do you write with the intention it will be used again (for example a recipe or a friend's new telephone number)?
- Would all your written communication make sense to everyone? Why/why not?
- If you record your thoughts, is it to explore a new idea or consolidate thinking?

The activity should have helped you to think about how written communication takes different forms for different purposes and for different audiences. Written work in mathematics should be no different. When you are planning, think about the purpose and audience of the children's work and identify the best way for children to record (if they need to at all). When you are confident in this, move on to the children choosing the way they will record their mathematics themselves.

Verbal communication

We identified in the word problem activity earlier that the teacher did not appear to be developing a classroom where talk was encouraged. Yet, Vygotsky (1987, page 280) explains how:

> *external speech is not inner speech plus sound any more than inner is external speech minus sound. The transition from inner to external speech is complex and dynamic. It is the transformation of a predicative, idiomatic speech into the syntax of differentiated speech which is comprehensible to others.*

Furthermore, John-Steiner and Mahn (2003, page 146) explain how individual cognitive change:

> *evolve[s] from the sustained dynamic of individuals engaged in symbolic behaviour both with other humans, present and past, and with material and non-material culture captured in books, artifacts and living memory.*

Despite a long-standing belief and understanding of the power of talking, many teachers continue to use more traditional didactic methods of teaching, as the research focus below demonstrates.

Research Focus

In the Independent Review of Mathematics Teaching in Early Years Settings and Primary Schools, Sir Peter Williams offered a number of recommendations for the long-term to *enhance the standing of the teaching profession and the mathematical learning of the children in their care* (Williams, 2008, page 4). One of the issues raised was the need for high-quality talk in mathematics. Williams explains how *the vitally important question of the classroom discussion of mathematics* is an issue he singles out. He states, *it is often suggested that 'mathematics itself is a language' but it must not be overlooked that only by constructive dialogue in the medium of the English language in the classroom can logic and reasoning be fully developed – the factors at the very heart of embedded learning in mathematics* (Williams, 2008, page 4).

Neil Mercer and his colleagues have undertaken research that tries to address the issues surrounding mathematical talk in primary classrooms and early years settings. They identified that:

● the teacher has a key role in enabling children to talk and reason together effectively;

● providing children with guidance and practice in how to use language for reasoning enables them to use it more effectively as a tool for working on mathematics problems together;

→

- improving the quality of children's use of language improves individuals' learning also;

- the teacher is an important model and guide for children's use of language and reasoning.

(Littleton *et al.*, 2005; Mercer and Sams, 2006a, 2006b)

Links to the National Curriculum

We can see here the core role that communication has, not just in mathematics, but across the whole of the school curriculum.

Some skills are universal, for example the skills of communication, improving own learning and performance, and creative thinking. These skills are also embedded in the subjects of the National Curriculum and are essential to effective learning.

(DfES, 1999, page 20)

Written communication

The Framework for Mathematics (DfE, 1999) went some way to highlight for teachers ways in which written work can develop across the primary age range. For example, teachers were encouraged to introduce number lines and move children towards using them more flexibly as empty number lines. Additionally, strategies such as partitioning were steps used on the way to recording more 'formal' algorithms. The QCA's (1999) *Teaching written calculations* booklet was instrumental in unpacking many of the methods in the Framework, linking together the expectations in the Framework with the underpinning rationale for the suggested written methods. It stated that the reasons for using written methods include:

- *to assist in a mental calculation by writing down some of the numbers involved;*
- *to clarify a mental procedure for the writer;*
- *to help to communicate solutions and methods with other readers;*
- *to provide a record of work done for themselves, teachers or others;*
- *to work out calculations which are too difficult to be done mentally;*
- *to develop, refine and use a set of rules for correct and efficient calculations.*

(QCA, 1999, page 3)

The research below might encourage you to consider how you might use diagrams as a method of written communication to help children to solve problems.

Research Focus

Pantziara *et al.*'s (2009) research explored the use of diagrams for solving non-routine problems. They define a diagram as *a visual representation that presents information in a spatial layout* (page 40). They identify within the research literature that:

- diagrams have been found to be one of the most effective strategies for improving the efficiency of solving problems;

- some children are unfamiliar with using diagrams in problem-solving, or cannot see the process in a diagrammatic way;

- diagrams presented to children change the nature of the problem (because a presented diagram provides a problem from the problem-setter's perspective, not the child's interpretation of the problem) but when children have struggled to create their own diagram, a presented diagram helps them to solve the problem;

- self-constructed diagrams provide a powerful problem-solving strategy because they offer a problem structure;

- when diagrams are constructed, they often help to identify unsolved parts of a problem or provide links between two pieces of given information;

- the diagram offers a knowledge system that provides the context to generate further information;

- diagrams support visual reasoning, rather than linguistic reasoning;

- children in grades 3–5 often have difficulty in identifying the type of diagram they should use.

Up until this point, written communication has referred to those jottings and procedures that might be undertaken using a pencil on paper. However, we would like to pause here to encourage you to think about how written communication can also be achieved using other methods of technology. For example, a spreadsheet can record numbers and formulae and show pattern. A calculator can hold certain numbers while others are used to calculate the solution of a more complex equation. A word processor can record a logically developing solution to a problem and be amended efficiently as necessary.

Links to the National Curriculum

The breadth of study for mathematics encourages children to: explore and use a variety of resources and materials, including ICT (1f), decide when to use a calculator (1g) and to use mathematics in other subjects.

What does communication involve?

We believe that communicating mathematics involves:

- accepting and giving feedback (including peer coaching);
- *ad hoc* as well as more structured representation;
- calculations;
- demonstrating reasoning;
- diagrams;
- explaining methods and solutions;
- ICT;
- lists;
- making choices and decisions;
- pictures;
- resources;
- tables;
- using mental images and models;
- written skills.

Learning Outcomes Review

This chapter began by outlining how it is essential for all people to possess a bank of mathematics skills in order to engage in the world around them. As a trainee teacher, it is your role to be able to recognise mathematics in all subjects and other parts of the school day. By drawing out mathematical experiences during lessons, children will be able to recognise and appreciate mathematics and in turn become confident young mathematicians who possess a positive mathematical disposition. The remainder of the chapter identified the three mathematical skills that are used and applied across the National Curriculum: reasoning, problem solving and communication. We defined each of these in their broadest terms. This sets the framework for the remaining chapters where we support you in furthering your knowledge and understanding about using and applying mathematics across the curriculum and in your own work as a trainee teacher.

Self-assessment questions

1. Why do you think mathematics is often taught as a discrete lesson and not integrated as other subjects might more easily be?

2. Identify five mathematical skills, knowledge or understanding you have used and applied in the last 24 hours.
3. Why does Ma1: Using and applying mathematics not have its own discrete programme of study (PoS) with objectives listed as the other PoS do?
4. What are the three skills in Ma1: Using and applying mathematics?
5. What key skills and thinking skills in the National Curriculum (pages 20–22) can you associate with Using and applying mathematics?
6. What subject(s) do not relate to mathematics or use mathematical skills in any way?

Further Reading

Claxton, G. (2008) *What's the point of school? Rediscovering the heart of education*. Oxford: Oneworld. This may challenge your own perceptions of the current state of education.

Mason, J. and Johnston-Wilder, S. (2006) *Designing and using mathematical tasks*. Maidenhead: Open University Press. This book encourages readers to look beyond mathematics as a cut-and-dried subject and to understand problem-solving and learning in a more powerful way.

National Centre for Excellent in the Teaching of Mathematics (NCETM) aims to support and encourage mathematics CPD. Visit **https://www.ncetm.org.uk/** to learn more.

NRICH aims to enrich the mathematical experiences of all learners. Visit **http://nrich.maths.org/public/** to find a plethora of tasks and activities that resonate with the underpinning philosophy of this book.

QCA (1999) *Teaching written calculation strategies*, available at **http://orderline.qcda.gov.uk/gempdf/1847213545.pdf** This is a useful resource to develop your understanding of when and why you should encourage children to use a range of written methods.

References

Bergqvist, E. (2007) Types of reasoning required in university exams in mathematics. *Journal of Mathematical Behaviour*, 26 (4): 348–370.

Boesen, J., Leithner, J. and Palm, T. (2010) The relation between types of assessment tasks and the mathematical reasoning students use. *Educational Studies in Mathematics*, 75: 89–105.

Bottage, B.A., Stephens, A.C., Rueda, E., Laroque, P.T. and Grant, T.S. (2010) Anchoring problem-solving and computation instruction in context-rich learning environments. *Exceptional Children*, 76 (4): 417–437.

Campos, D.G. (2010) Peirce's philosophy of mathematical education: Fostering reasoning abilities for mathematical inquiry. *Studies in Philosophy and Education*, 29: 421–439.

Department for Education and Employment (1999) *Mathematics. The National Curriculum for England: Key Stages 1–4*. London: DfEE Publications.

Department for Education and Skills (2003) Mathematics framework available at **http:// nationalstrategies.standards.dcsf.gov.uk/primary/primaryframework/mathematics framework**

Fuchs, L.S., Fuchs, D., Stuebing, K., Fletcher, J.M., Hamlett, C.L. and Lambert, W. (2008) Problem solving and computational skill: Are they shared or distinct aspects of mathematical cognition? *Journal of Educational Psychology*, 100 (1): 30–47.

Green, K.H and Emerson, A. (2010) Mathematical reasoning in service courses: Why students need mathematical modelling problems. *Montana Mathematics Enthusiast*, 7 (1): 113–140.

Hanna, G. (2000) Factors in the decline of proof. *Interchange*, 31 (1): 21–33.

Heibert, J. (2003) What research says about the NCTM standards. In J. Kilpatrick, G. Martin, and D. Schifter (eds) *A Research Companion to Principles and Standards for School Mathematics* (pages 5–23). Reston: National Council of Teachers of Mathematics.

Hélie, S. and Sun, R. (2010) Incubation, insight, and creative problem solving: A unified theory and a connectionist model. *Psychological Review*, 117 (3): 994–1024.

HMI (2002) Teaching of calculation in primary schools. London: HMI. Available at **www.ofsted.gov.uk/Ofsted-home/Publications-and-research/Browse-all-by/Education/ Curriculum/Mathematics/Primary/Teaching-of-calculation-in-primary-schools** (accessed 1/ 3/11).

Inhelder, B. and Piaget, J. (1958) *The growth of logical thinking from childhood to adolescence*. New York: Basic Books.

Jenkins, P. and Lyle, S. (2010) Enacting dialogue: the impact of promoting philosophy for children on the literate thinking of identified poor readers, aged 10. *Language and Education: An International Journal*, 24 (6): 459–472.

John-Steiner, V. and Mahn, H. (2003) Sociocultural contexts for teaching and learning. In W.M. Reynolds and G.E. Miller (eds) *Handbook of Pyschology* (pages 125–151). Hoboken, NJ: Wiley.

Kramarski, B. and Revach, T. (2009) The challenge of self-regulated learning in mathematics teachers' professional training. *Educational Studies in Mathematics*, 73 (3): 379–399.

Littleton, K., Mercer, N., Dawes, L., Wegerif, R., Rowe, D. and Sams, C. (2005) Talking and thinking together at Key Stage 1. *Early Years*, 25 (2): 167–182.

Mercer, N. and Sams, C. (2006a) The analysis of classroom talk: Methods and methodologies. *British Journal of Educational Psychology*, 80 (1): 1–14.

Mercer, N. and Sams, C. (2006b) Teaching children how to use language to solve maths problems. *Language and Education: An International Journal,* 20 (6): 507–528.

National Council of Teachers of Mathematics (2000) *Principles and standards for school mathematics.* Reston, VA: National Council of Teachers of Mathematics.

National Strategies (2010) Developing mathematics in initial teacher training. Available at **www.nationalstrategies.standards.dcsf.gov.uk/node/461819** (accessed 1/5/11).

Nunes, T., Bryant, P., Evans, D., Bell, D., Gardner, S., Gardner A. and Carraher, J. (2007) The contribution of logical reasoning to the learning of mathematics in primary school. *British Journal of Developmental Psychology,* 25: 147–166.

Palm, T. (2008) Impact of authenticity on sense making in word problem solving. *Educational Studies in Mathematics,* 67 (1): 37–58.

Pantziara, M., Gagatsis, A. and Elia, I. (2009) Using diagrams as tools for the solution of non-routine mathematical problems. *Educational Studies in Mathematics,* 72 (1): 39–60.

Sarama, J., and Clements, D.H. (2009a) Teaching math in the primary grades: The learning trajectories approach. *Young Children,* 64 (2): 63–65.

Sarama, J. and Clements, D. (2009b) *Early childhood mathematics education research: Learning trajectories for young children.* New York: Routledge.

Stylianides, A.J. (2007) Proof and proving in school mathematics. *Journal for Research in Mathematics Education,* 38: 289–321.

Thorndike, E. (1922) *The psychology of arithmetic.* New York: Macmillan.

Topping, K. J., Campbell, J., Douglas, W. and Smith, A. (2003) Cross-age tutoring in mathematics with seven- and 11-year olds: Influence on mathematical vocabulary, strategic dialogue and self-concept. *Educational Research,* 45 (3): 287–308.

Watson, S. (2008) *How do Astronauts Eat in Space?* HowStuffWorks.com. **http://science.howstuffworks.com/astronauts-eat-in-space.htm** (accessed 23/2/11).

Williams, P. (2008) Independent review of mathematics teaching in early years settings and primary schools. Final Report. DfES. Available at **www.education.gov.uk/publications/eOrderingDownload/WMR%20Final%20Report.pdf** (accessed 20/3/11).

Wisegeek.com *What foods do astronauts eat in space?* **www.wisegeek.com/what-foods-do-astronauts-eat-in-space.htm** (accessed 1/5/11).

Yackel, E. and Hanna, G. (2003) Reasoning and proof. In J. Kilpatrick, G. Martin and D. Schifter (eds) *A research companion to principles and standards for school mathematics* (pages 227–236). Reston: National Council of Teachers of Mathematics.

2. Number

Learning Outcomes

This chapter explores:
- early origins of number;
- our present place value system;
- imperial and metric number;
- use of appropriate language to teach number;
- mathematics trails;
- number in music and dance;
- money.

Professional Standards for QTS

Q3 (a) Be aware of the professional duties of teachers and the statutory framework within which they work.

Q8 Have a creative and constructively critical approach towards innovation, being prepared to adapt their practice where benefits and improvements are identified.

Q14 Have a secure knowledge and understanding of their subjects/curriculum areas and related pedagogy to enable them to teach effectively across the age and ability range for which they are trained.

Q15 Know and understand the relevant statutory and non-statutory curricula and frameworks, including those provided through the National Strategies, for their subjects/curriculum areas, and other relevant initiatives applicable to the age and ability range for which they are trained.

Q23 Design opportunities for learners to develop their literacy, numeracy and ICT skills.

Q25 Teach lessons and sequences of lessons across the age and ability range for which they are trained in which they:

(a) Use a range of teaching strategies and resources, including e-learning, taking practical account of diversity and promoting equality and inclusion.

(c) Adapt their language to suit the learners they teach, introducing new ideas and concepts clearly, and using explanations, questions, discussions and plenaries effectively.

Q30 Establish a purposeful and safe learning environment conducive to learning and identify opportunities for learners to learn in out-of-school contexts.

Introduction

Chapter 1 discussed how reasoning, problem-solving and communication are the essential skills children need to be able to reflect upon and discuss their work and its quality, and develop their understanding about what they can do to improve it. This chapter will concentrate on how these skills are used in the learning of number from a mathematical perspective and how number can aid the learning of other subject areas.

The need to use and apply number

First concepts of number date back to the Palaeolithic age but it wasn't until the New Stone Age that numerical terms started to be developed as humans developed from hunter-gatherer to producer. As settlements developed, crafts such as carpentry, baking, pottery and smelting also developed. People gained more possessions, and the need to check these became important, hence the need to be able to count. In today's world we are surrounded by the written word and numbers form a large part of this. However, not all numbers are used for the purpose of counting.

In Chapter 1 you were asked to think of the mathematical skills involved in everyday tasks such as deciding what to wear and setting the alarm clock. This activity may have surprised you in as much as you were not aware of all the mathematics that is 'hidden' within our everyday lives. This would seem to beg the question of whether something needs a label for it to be that thing (i.e. is it mathematics because we label it as such?) and so the debate and discussion for combining different subjects across the curriculum begins.

We would now like you to think about a typical day and consider how and where you might encounter number in whatever form.

Activity

The table below is the start of a list of numbers that you might see on any given day. Try to add to the list and complete the 'purpose' column

Type of number	Purpose
Car registration plate	
Clock face	
Road signs	
Door numbers	
Postcodes	
Price tags	
Shoe size	
Clothes size	

Did you find that once you started to think about this you were able to add more and more types of number? Perhaps you have never thought about numbers in this way before, but as you will discover on placement, children are very observant and will notice much of the world around us that adults simply miss. They will ask questions beginning with *Why...?* For example, *Why are my shoes size 13 and my Dad's are size 8, but his feet are much bigger than mine?* A tricky question to answer, if this has never occurred to you and you have no idea how shoes are sized.

By asking you to complete the 'purpose' column our intention was for you to start to appreciate the importance of encouraging children to communicate, reason and problem-solve if they are to begin to understand the world around them.

Do we really use a decimal system?

Professor Alison Wolf (DfES, 1999, page 61) argues that *maths is a truly global language. With it, we convey ideas to each other that words can't handle – and bypass our spoken Tower of Babel.* While this can certainly be said to be true once children begin to use symbols to represent number, the terminology used to describe quantity can still be a source of confusion.

Although the language used for counting has developed over time and some words may not still be in use, some still remain and are in common use to this day.

Activity

Consider the following list. What quantity does each word refer to? How many of these words do you use in everyday conversation?

dozen

score

couple

century

gross

myriad

pair

brace

Some of the words may have been more familiar to you than others. Perhaps as you read through the list, words such as 'couple' or 'pair' triggered images of people and so it was easier to relate these words to the quantity of 2. Words such as 'score' may have been a little more difficult to quantify as this word is used when referring to many different quantities. For example 'The score was Liverpool 4, Arsenal 2'. In fact as a quantity a 'score' is 20. 'Three score years and ten' was for many years regarded as the life expectancy of people in the Western world. Do you think this is still the case? If not, how would you now describe life expectancy in terms of 'score'?

The activity illustrates that assumptions are often made regarding children's prior knowledge. Words that we use to explain a task may be interpreted by the child to mean something completely different. Noss and Hoyles (1996) explain how learners use formal and informal resources to construct mathematical meaning by making and reinforcing links between these resources. These resources are both internal (cognitive) and external (physical or virtual). Learners abstract within rather than away from (*ab-stract*) a situation, webbing their own knowledge and understanding by acting within the situation. Once children hear the word, they search their internal resources looking for triggers solving the problem and comprehending the meaning of the word. Sometimes children reason internally and then communicate verbally only to discover they are incorrect. We call these misconceptions.

The use of terminology related to quantity can often be misleading. Imagine a child learning facts related to the number 2. He has just learned that the word 'couple' means two and has mastered the skill of telling the time. The teacher is working with him and needs to speak to another child on the other side of the classroom. She tells him not to move and says she will be 'a couple of minutes'. Full of enthusiasm and pride that he understands what she has just said the child is happy to follow the minute hand of his new watch while it completes two revolutions. Unfortunately the teacher is a great deal longer coming back and wonders why the child is upset. He explains that he thought 'a couple' meant two and that she took ten minutes to come back. She replies, *I meant I wouldn't be long*. The child is now confused. Does couple mean 'two' or does it mean 'not very long'?

Using metric and imperial numbers

The metric system was legally recognised in France in 1799 and became mandatory in 1840 (Spiering, 2001). However, it was only in the 1970s when decimalisation was introduced in Britain that our monetary system changed to base 10, and so the need to be able to calculate using base 12 and base 20 was redundant. The metric system introduced kilometres, metres, centimetres and millimetres to the measuring system and again the need to be able to calculate using base 12 was lost. However, it is common practice in many primary schools to insist that children still learn the times tables to 12×12 and children are still expected to be able to convert from one decimal unit to another and from metric to imperial.

If you think for a moment of life beyond the classroom you will begin to realise that much use of number is still imperial. Next time you are on a flight listen carefully to the pilot and you may hear him announce how many thousand feet the plane is flying at. Petrol is still referred to in gallons, beer in pints and road signs refer to distance in miles. When children talk about their height they use feet and inches and weight in stones and ounces. These examples would seem to reinforce the confusion for children and strengthen the belief that mathematics is something separate from other subjects and from our everyday lives, and that mathematics is something that we only 'do' in school (MacGregor, 2002). Using and applying mathematics – and being explicit about it with the children – in all curriculum subjects goes some way to addressing this myth. The history curriculum includes a study of Britain since 1930 and children are encouraged to recognise and understand the lives of the people at the time. This is often achieved by role-play when children will need to understand imperial units but in the context of comparison and conversion with metric units. This idea is developed later in this chapter.

How well do you understand imperial numbers? The following problems are all taken from *Mental arithmetic – Problems for juniors, Book 4*, by E. and N.L. Bradbury (1960) and would have been the kind of questions given to 7–11 year-olds.

Activity

As you attempt this activity note down the strategies that you use and how you might use this knowledge to understand how children begin to learn and develop strategies for calculating. You might need the following information.

/-	Symbol for shilling
d	Symbol for pence
2/8	Is read as 2 shillings and 8 pence
£1 1/-	Equivalent to one guinea

1. Write in figures the number which is a quarter of sixteen thousand and sixteen.
2. What change will there be from 5/- after buying 1 3/4lbs of steak at 2/8 a lb?
3. How many yards are there in a one mile race?
4. Tom is 9. His father is 4 times Tom's age and his grandfather is twice as old as Tom's father. What is the sum of their ages?
5. How much would a housewife pay for twenty bags of coke at 5/6 a bag?
6. Find the sum of prime numbers between 10 and 20.
7. How many 2 pint cans of paraffin can be filled from a 20 gallon drum?
8. Mrs Jones spent 10 guineas on a coat. If this was 7/12 of the money she had saved, how much did she start with?

How did you get on? Was there more information that you felt you needed? Were some questions easier than others?

Taking a cross-curricular approach means involving children understanding and making sense of the world around them. The questions above would probably have been considered 'real life' problems at the time and children would have been expected to complete them on their own in silence. Reflect on your own experience teaching word problems. What are the similarities and differences from your experience?

The activity you have just completed may lead you to think that conversion is something that only happens between past and present number. However, the following research focus reminds us that today there are still a number of cultural differences in the way that we present and use number.

Research Focus: Cultural differences

Greiffenhagen and Sharrock (2006) identify how there are cultural differences in the way number is present and counting is carried out. They illustrate this with the following examples.

In French, *quatrevingt* is used for 80, which is translated (or represented) as 4×20. Of course in English we would say 'eighty' (8×10). (For further discussion about the use of number in French, see Chapter 4.)

In English number, we group digits in threes and label them thousands. However, in Chinese, four digits are grouped together to be ten thousands, or *wan*. So 50,000 would be 'fifty thousand' ($50 \times 1,000$) in English but '*wu wan*' ($5 \times 10,000$) in Chinese.

The Oksapmin people who live in the mountainous regions of Papua New Guinea used a 27-part body counting system up until the 1940s.

Greiffenhagen and Sharrock (2006, page 98) explain how *these (and many, many more) are examples of cultural variation in mathematical practices. However, they are despite their differences also readily recognizable as diverse forms of mathematics and relatively easy to translate, coordinate, and learn.*

Communicating number

Historically, communication was the forerunner to the written word. This is mirrored in child development. From a very early age children begin to make sense of the world around them by talking long before they are confident recorders and writers, and use language to discuss and express number. Before children have mastered the spoken word they try desperately to be understood by the noises that they make. They even try to use expression by changing the tone and level of these noises, often resulting in frustration and exasperation for both themselves and the listener. Once they have mastered the spoken word they try to begin to make sense of it. You will often hear people ask pre-school aged children how old they are. They will proudly give an answer, for example '4', but then when they are asked how old mum or dad is they will cheerfully give what seems a completely inaccurate number such as '12' or '100' (Levene *et al.*, 2010). This suggests that although they know or have been told how old they are, their ability to understand what this number means has yet to be developed. As mentioned previously, ask children their height and they will give an answer in feet and inches. They understand that it is a quantity and are happy to use terminology. It is this sense of number and mathematical disposition and application to any given situation that needs to be nurtured and developed in order for deeper understanding to take place. Children need to begin to understand the meaning behind the words or labels given to the symbols we know as numbers.

Using story to communicate number

Before children begin formal schooling they will encounter number in many different situations in the world around them. One of the first ways that children will do this is through nursery rhymes and stories (Gifford, 2004).

Table 2.1 lists some examples of the many books that could be used in school or at home to help children develop their ideas of number used for counting.

Title	Author
1,2,3 to the zoo	Eric Carle
Counting on an elephant	Jill McDonald
Goldilocks and the three bears	T Bradman
Mr Magnolia	Quentin Blake
One bear all alone	C Bucknall
Ten in a bed	Penny Dale
Ten little mice	Joyce Dunbar
The boy who was followed home	Margaret Mahy

Table 2.1 List of children's books that can be used to support children's understanding of number and counting

Research Focus: Using story in mathematics

In a research study from the United States, Kinniburgh and Byrd (2008) used *Ten black dots* as a resource in a social studies (geography and history) and mathematics unit learning about the events of 11 September 2001 with older elementary children.

They identify how using story can:

- create a positive environment for learning mathematics;
- bring mathematics to life in the classroom;
- make the abstract become concrete;
- engage children who suffer from mathematics anxiety;
- show children that mathematics is not a discrete subject carried out once a day in isolation, but that it is a crucial component of life;

→

- involve stories that are beyond the recommended reading level of the children being taught;
- integrate mathematics and other subjects effectively.

To read more about using books to develop mathematical understanding, or to use and apply mathematics in geometry, refer to the Research Focus 'Story bags' in Chapter 3.

Mathematical content in stories is not a new idea. Lewis Carroll published *Alice's adventures in wonderland* in 1865. This story is based entirely on mathematical concepts such as symmetry, scale, time, etc. When you are considering using books to teach mathematics or to use mathematics to teach another subject, ensure that the connections are *authentic, not contrived; they should help children learn to think about mathematical ideas as ways of expressing relationships rather than discrete bits of information to be memorized and retrieved* (Hellwig *et al.*, 2000, page 138).

Questions present opportunities for children and their teacher

Chapter 1 outlined your role as a trainee teacher in ensuring you offer opportunity for children to talk. This section now asks you to focus specifically on one type of talk – asking questions. Having an awareness of children posing questions throughout the school day will help you to:

- develop a class ethos where asking questions is expected and rewarded, and develops each child as a learner and co-teacher;
- encourage children to ask questions they are genuinely interested in, rather than those they think you expect them to ask;
- find out what they know and what to find out;
- what they are interested in;
- draw on their interests to use interesting contexts for your planning;
- offer an opportunity for your children to be motivated to learn by the context provided, and them driving the learning agenda.

Activity
Using the number 6 as an answer, list 30 questions that could be asked to elicit that answer.

While you are completing the task, think about the following questions.
- What contexts are you using?
- What mathematical patterns are you drawing upon?
- How could you use this task in school?

> • What richer information would you gather from the children if they were
> undertaking a task of this type, rather than, say, a worksheet where they were to
> complete the answers?

So, what questions did you ask?

Perhaps you wrote:

6 + 0
5 + 1
4 + 2
3 + 3
2 + 4
1 + 5
0 + 6

If so, did you continue the pattern? For example, what about:

$-1 + 7$
$-2 + 8$?

Did you use a variety of mathematical vocabulary? What about 'double 3', or 'one quarter of 24'? Did you use everyday contexts, such as 'half a dozen'?

Children asking questions themselves reveals a lot more about their mathematical understanding and, crucially, their ability to use and apply mathematics in a range of other subject contexts. This also gives you an opportunity to assess the children's mathematical attainment, providing useful data for you to use. You can read more about this latter point in Chapter 7.

Mathematics trails

A recurring theme throughout this book is to engage children in meaningful learning linked to the world around them. Many curriculum subjects lend themselves to study outside the classroom such as the study of rivers and map reading in geography, or the Victorian classroom in history. In mathematics, trails are an opportunity to exploit the outdoors. In a previous activity you were asked to think about the purpose of number that we encounter in our everyday lives. The following case study shows how a trainee mathematics specialist created a mathematics trail to link this activity with geography, ICT and English. As you read it you might like to think how you can use your learning and assessment requirements from your studies to enhance your placement experience.

Case Study: Maths trails in Year 2

Carole is a final-year mathematics specialist. As part of her specialism assignment she is required to show how mathematics and another subject can be taught together to complement each other. She decides to combine geography and mathematics by producing a mathematics trail of the town in which her next placement school is situated. The intention is twofold. One is to complete her assignment and the other is to prepare a resource that she will be able to use on placement.

She begins by walking round the local area and taking digital photos of all the examples of number that she can find. She collects leaflets and menus from restaurants and shops, before creating a booklet of instructions and questions.

On the day of the trail each child is given a booklet and a town map and assigned to a supervising adult. Some parts of the questions are to be completed as the trail proceeds while others are to be completed once the children are back in the classroom. Once the trail has been undertaken the children return to school. Carole then explains that they are going to use all the information they have to create a large town map for display in the classroom.

The map is produced and the pictures of the various places they have visited are fixed around the outside with arrows indicating where they are on the map. The menus, leaflets and children's answers to the questions are used to create role-play areas such as a café and post office. Reception children are invited to use these with the Year 2 children taking the orders and working out the prices, etc.

This map is left up long after Carole has finished her placement and the class teacher is able to extend the ideas further. Children find their houses on the map, take pictures of each other and work out who lives nearest/furthest away from school and produce a sequence of pictures along the wall showing distance away from school.

Carole is able to use her observations of the children and evidence of their work to complete her assignment. She is also able to adapt and improve her resource based on her own reflection and discussion with the class teacher.

Any time you take children out of school grounds you will need to be aware of the health and safety implications and you will discuss this with your class teacher. In Chapter 6 you will read more about planning a school trip. In the above case study, Carole had carried out a visit to the town to complete the intended route of the trail. She had noted down all the potential hazards before deciding the optimum time to take the children. She ensured that she had the correct amount of assistance from other adults and had informed parents/carers.

Links to the National Curriculum

By combining mathematics, geography and ICT Carole has been able to cover many of the programmes of study in each subject. By giving children the booklet of questions to be answered both on the trail and after, she has taken into account elements of counting, number patterns and sequences, the number system, calculations and solving numerical problems (Ma2). Taking photos and using them to record information for retrieval has addressed areas of ICT such as *gathering information from a variety of sources* (1a), *retrieving information that has been stored* (1c) and *working with a range of information to investigate the different ways it can be presented* (5a). Encouraging children to identify where their house is and the different places in relation to school addresses knowledge and understanding in geography (3b) and brings in some of the elements of the breadth of study such as *the locality of the school* (6a) and *carry out fieldwork investigation outside the classroom* (7b).

Activity

Below is a sample of the questions included in Carole's mathematics trail for Key Stage 1. Try to add at least one more question to each group.

A Maths Trail for Key Stage 1

Look at the manhole cover in the playground.
- Can you find what year it was made?
- Can you use any of the digits on the plate to make your age?

Look up on the wall. There is an alarm on the wall.
- What is the telephone number on it?
- The telephone number makes two, five-digit numbers. Take the smallest number from the biggest number and what do you get?

Look at the windows on the church hall.
- How many panes were used to make one window?
- How many rectangles do you see in your picture?

Ticket machine in the car park
- How much does it cost to park a car for 1 hour?
- What coins does it accept?
- What is the least number of coins you can use for this?

Post office
- What are the opening hours of the post office?
- Are the opening hours the same for each day?

Health centre
- How many more hours is the health centre open on a Monday than a Friday?

> • Look at the telephone number. What is the largest number you can make using the digits in the telephone number? What is the smallest number you can make?

What did you notice about the types of questions asked? Some were closed questions, with one correct answer, but others offered an opportunity to investigate mathematical ideas.

Research Focus: Mathematics trails

Tsao (2010) focused on integrating mathematics trails into her teaching with Grade 6 children. She explains that mathematical trails are a dynamic rather than static learning experience for children. Tsao found that the mathematics problems the children were presented with on the trail were unique, so the related questions could not be found elsewhere. By undertaking mathematics trails, she found that the children gained the feeling that they were experiencing mathematically related objects in their everyday surroundings. She also observed how the children had an increased interest in mathematics and in turn this improved their attainment. Tsao cites Lin (2002) who identifies that mathematics trails (a) provide the opportunity to practise thinking; (b) provide a supplementary teaching resource for teachers; (c) consolidate knowledge and skills; (d) connect life-school contexts; and (e) develop communication skills.

Tsao provides practical advice for setting up a mathematics trail, stating that we should consider playfulness, the opportunity for mathematical thinking and making connections, as well as inclusion within the trail. She also suggests (page 84) that when designing the trail, it is necessary to:

- clarify the mathematical purpose of the trail;
- know the children's attainment levels and read related literature;
- carefully select and explore the environment;
- plan the route, with timings;
- think about the mathematical questions and transform them to the environment;
- trial, evaluate and modify the trail.

Music and dance

Pythagoras was a Greek mathematician who lived in the 500s BC. He believed that beauty and harmony could be explained by numbers. He recognised the mathematical relationship between the pitch of a sound and the length of a string or pipe, or the size of a bell. He discovered that halving the length of a string doubles the frequency of its fundamental vibration, and raises the pitch by an octave.

Harmonics are the different frequencies at which something can vibrate. A string stretched between two supports can vibrate so that the varying numbers of wavelengths fit along the string. The wave with the longest wavelength is called the fundamental. Other vibrations have shorter wavelengths and higher frequencies. This progressive series of frequencies is known as harmonics. The proportion of different harmonics gives an instrument its individual sound.

It is said that good mathematicians make good musicians and vice versa as both disciplines call for the need to count, sequence and follow pattern (Tan and Chua, 2006). Certainly closer examination of the two subjects uncovers a good deal of overlap in areas such as fractions and pattern.

Table 2.2 below gives a few examples of the link between the two disciplines.

Music	Mathematics
Time signatures	Fractions
Note values	Number and fractions
Sound waves	Frequency (Hz)
String harmonics	Proportion
Musical scale	Sequence
Repeats	Pattern

Table 2.2 Links between music and mathematics

Learning a new song or dance will involve a great deal of counting. Many classrooms in years gone by and perhaps still today use rhythmic rote learning of tables. While this can be effective for aiding instant recall of facts, it could be argued that for some it is in fact simply learning a song. Repetition can certainly trigger recall. How often do you find yourself singing to the music on the radio and apparently knowing all the words without ever having actually learned them? However, if you were asked to begin the song in the middle or without hearing the tune, you may struggle. The same can be true for children and the tables when asked to recall answers in a different sequence to the tables 'song' they have learned.

When learning a new dance the steps are broken down into the component parts and assigned numbers. As the dance is learned the reliance on counting fades and the memory takes over so that when the music starts instant recall takes place.

As you read the case study below think about your own preferred styles of learning. Perhaps you are like many people who say they cannot sing or dance and find the thought of teaching these things to children quite daunting. If so, think about the strategies you can use to encourage the children to compose and think about rhythm.

Case Study: The Christmas play

Geraldine is a music specialist trainee on her final placement. The school is keen to use her expertise to help with the school Christmas play. The head teacher is a pianist and plays the violin to a high standard. He has written some original music for the Year 2 children to perform, but is finding it hard going as the children cannot grasp that different notes last for differing amounts of time. He explains this to Geraldine and she takes on the challenge by deciding to plan a day that combines maths, music and English. As she is still learning the children's names she begins the day with the children sitting in a circle. She explains that they are going to take it in turns to say their names in time with the beat but that they have to break them down into syllables, for example, John, Pa – trick, Rose – ma – ry. Once the children have managed this they work in small groups to compose a brief compilation of their names to perform to the rest of the class. John and Patrick are really keen to perform their composition:

Pa – trick, Pa – trick, Pa – trick, John
Pa – trick, Pa – trick, Pa – trick, John
Pa – trick, Pa – trick, Pa – trick, John
Pa – trick, Pa – trick, Pa – trick, John
Pa – trick, Pa – trick, Pa – trick, John
Pa – trick, Pa – trick, Pa – trick, John

After they have performed, Geraldine asks them why they have chosen that pattern and they explain that when they started saying their names they realised that it sounded like 'Twinkle, twinkle, little star' so then they knew where each name should go.

The other children start to say their names and immediately start to recognise tunes that they know. Pleased that they are able to keep a rhythm going, Geraldine gives them some laminated musical notes and explains that each note represents a length of time and are called crotchets, quavers and semiquavers. The children learn that the value of these are one note, half a note and a quarter of a note respectively. She shows them how to clap out a steady beat and then they are able to create their own music using the notes and the values correctly.

As the children become more familiar with the idea of note length, Geraldine gradually gives some of the children chime bars and replaces clapping with playing the notes. The others are encouraged to listen to the beat and begin to make up dance steps in time to the beat. By the end of the afternoon the children are ready to perform their own music and dance steps and later in the week they start to attempt the head teacher's composition and preparation for the Christmas play has begun.

The case study shows clearly how children try to use prior knowledge to help with present tasks. John and Patrick were able to recognise the rhythm of a song they already knew and replace the words with their names. In Chapter 6 you will read more about fitting different components into the timetable and ensuring that all subjects are afforded appropriate time over the year. Things such as plays and performances are important aspects of any primary school and help to develop a holistic approach to learning. By engaging the children in the process of preparing a performance they are more likely to retain the skills than if they have simply been presented with the finished product.

Money

Money is often cited as one of the aspects of mathematics that trainee teachers find most difficult to teach. Teaching these concepts embedded in cross-curricular ways is a highly effective way to support children's knowledge, understanding and skills related to money (Lucey and Maxwell, 2009).

It is mooted that in today's society children do not know the value of money and are more used to seeing credit cards used for payment than notes and coins (Dudgeon and Hansen, 2011). If this really is the case then there is even more need for children to become familiar with our monetary system in school and understand its value and how this fits into the world around them. It is hardly surprising that children find money a confusing concept at times. Although we use the same symbols, i.e. 0–9 when writing down monetary calculations, we do not have the corresponding coins to match these values. There also appears to be no consistent or logical pattern for children to follow in order to gain a deeper understanding of these values (Tucker et al., 2010). Logic would suggest that as we have a £2 (200p) coin followed by a £1(100p) coin which is half of the £2, the next coin should be 50p which is half of the £1.

Continuing this logical thought process the next coin should be 25p but this would make the next 12½p. As we know this is not the case and instead we have 20p, 10p, 5p – again with a pattern of half – followed by 2p and 1p – also half.

Case Study: Using coins to explore historical ideas

Simon is a trainee teacher in Year 6. It has just been announced that there is to be a Royal Wedding and that everyone is going to have an additional bank holiday. This has caused great excitement in the class and much discussion has been had regarding kings and queens. Simon has recently inherited a large collection of coins and has brought them into school to show the children. They seem enthused by both the coins and the royal family so after discussion with his mentor, he decides to use this interest to plan a day of lessons making the coins the main resource, but also including coins in current use. As the content is going to be mixed he decides to give the day a theme rather than divide it into separate subjects. In his planning he makes the different learning objectives being covered for each subject clear along with his assessment criteria.

He begins by simply letting the children work together to sort the coins. Through discussion they are able to discover facts for themselves. Many begin by examining the coins and then notice that there are dates on them. They begin to lay them out in date order and discover that there are no coins with the present year but that one goes back to 1845.

As they feed back what they have discovered, Simon collates the information on a prepared interactive whiteboard document before asking the children what they would now like to know. He then adds this information and explains to the children how the table (Table 2.3) ensures they have a working document to use for the remainder of the day.

What we found out	What we would like to know
There are men's and women's heads on one side of the coins	Who are the people on the coins?
Some heads face left and some face right	Why do some heads face left and some face right?
The Queen's image is different – on some coins she is a girl and on some she is an older lady.	When does the image change? Does it change on all the coins at the same time? How long does a coin stay in circulation? How many coins are there in circulation? How are they collected in? When does a coin go out of date and not be legal tender?

→

There are different pictures on the other side of the coins	What are these? Who decides what is going onto the coins? Are they changed at the same time as the image on the other side?
The coins are different sizes and shapes	Do the shapes mean anything? Why aren't they all circular? Why is a five pence coin smaller than a one penny coin, but worth more?
The coins are different weights	Is the weight linked to the value of the coin?
The coins are different colours	What are the coins made of? Why are they different?
There are numbers on the coins	What do the numbers mean? Why don't we have a four pence coin?
Some of these are ones we use	How much are the old ones worth?
Some are really old	What is the oldest coin? What is the newest coin? When were the last coins minted? When will they be minted again? When was the first coin made? What did people use before coins? When was paper money invented?

Table 2.3 Exploring coins

The children choose who they would like to work with and, using the prompts from above, begin to source the answers to the questions. As the children search the internet and begin to find answers to one question they realise that the answers give rise to more questions. Through discussion they also realise that many of their grandparents may have used some of these old coins and ask Simon if they can develop these ideas further. They wanted to invite some older people into school to interview them about their lives as children and how they used this 'old' money.

Before long Simon realises that what had started as a chance question from one of the children has provided work that would cross much of the curriculum for the term. He works closely with the mentor to produce a valuable cross-curricular resource pack that will be kept by the school and used long after he had finished his placement.

Links to the National Curriculum

Through collaboration and discussion, children in the case study were able to improve and enhance their chronological understanding and historical interpretation. Using their knowledge of numbers and the number system they were able to compile questions, and talk about what information they need and how they can find and use it (ICT 1a). Once they had found this information they then decided how to prepare information for development using ICT, including selecting suitable sources, finding information, classifying it and checking it for accuracy (ICT 1b).

Bringing it all together

Throughout this book we are exploring how reasoning, problem-solving and communication are essential tools required to teach mathematics within other subjects and other subjects within mathematics. This next case study is an example of how subjects can be taught discretely but still be linked and what is learned in one can be used in another.

Case Study: Egypt

Ffinlo is a trainee teacher in a Year 3 class on his final placement. He has been asked by his class teacher if he has any idea how to try to incorporate mathematics with art and history. He remembers a session from one of his mathematics modules where many of the trainees were struggling to understand the need to link subjects or how to do it. The tutor had been aware of this and had adapted the session to try to help them. Ffinlo recalls:

Well, we were all really struggling to get to grips with the idea that subjects could be linked so she decided to show us by delivering a practical session where we all had to work together to plan a holiday.

We went to one of the computer rooms and once we sorted ourselves into groups we then had to decide where we wanted to go and how long for. After that it was down to us really. The only thing she did was give us a brief outline: You are going on holiday with your friends. You must produce an itemised list of train/air fares or petrol costs/car hire; times of departure and return and accommodation costs.

We all set off searching the internet for air fares to exotic places and posh hotels, hiring big cars and arranging to go to up-market restaurants every night. You know 'money no object' type of thing. I remember at one point looking round the room and thinking 'Wow! Everyone is working really hard' and the buzz in the room was amazing.

Half way through the session she stopped us and asked us how we were getting on and then said, 'Oh sorry I meant to say... You only have £700 to spend! So you will need to adjust your figures.'

$\rightarrow$

There were lots of groans but we were all so engaged with what we were doing that everyone began again, looking to see where they could reduce their costs. It was really funny at one point as one boy said very loudly to his mate, 'Well I'm sorry but we are going to have to share a double room 'cos it's 25 per cent cheaper and if we borrow a child we can get a reduction for a family!'

At the end of the session we were asked to note down all the skills that we had used and the subject areas we had covered to sort out our holiday. It was only then that we realised that we all do this kind of thing, but had never thought about it as being mathematics or geography. Maybe we could do something similar.

The class teacher liked this idea and together they planned and taught a sequence of lessons, beginning with a history session on the Ancient Egyptians looking at hieroglyphics. The next lesson was an art lesson reproducing the Egyptian numbers. A mathematics lesson followed on money and exchange rates before bringing all the skills and knowledge together and planning their own trip to Egypt using the ideas from Ffinlo's undergraduate taught session.

Learning Outcomes Review

This chapter has explored number from the early origins through to the present day. Imperial units have been compared to metric and an explanation offered as to why children and many adults to this day use a combination of both. We have stressed the need for appropriate language to be used in the teaching of number. Mathematics trails, music, dance and money have all been introduced as resources for helping children to learn, use and apply mathematics across the curriculum.

Self-assessment questions

1. How might providing the answer to a group of children, rather than a set of closed questions, encourage their use and application of number?
2. What are the benefits of using the outdoors as a learning environment?
3. Identify a link between poetry and music.
4. How might you use photographs of post boxes to explore history, in a similar way to the coins in the case study in this chapter?

Further Reading

Hansen, A. (2008) *Primary mathematics: Extending knowledge in practice.* Exeter: Learning Matters. This discusses Gelman and Gallistel's principles of counting in more detail.

Scieszka, J. and Smith, L. (2007) *Math Curse.* New York: Viking Children's Books. This is a children's story book that explores mathematical problem-solving.

References

Bradbury, E. and Bradbury, N.L. (1960) *Mental arithmetic – Problems for juniors.* Oxford: Basil Blackwell.

Capraro, R.M. and Capraro, M.M (2006) Are you really going to read us a story? Learning geometry through children's mathematics literature. *Reading Psychology,* 27 (1): 21–36.

Dudgeon, J. and Hansen, A. (2011) Measures, in Hansen, A. (ed.) *Children's errors in mathematics.* Exeter: Learning Matters, pages 99–121.

Gifford, S. (2004) A new mathematics pedagogy for the early years: In search of principles for practice. *International Journal of Early Years Education,* 12 (2): 99–115.

Greiffenhagen, C. and Sharrock, W. (2006) Mathematical relativism: Logic, grammar, and arithmetic in cultural comparison. *Journal for the Theory of Social Behaviour,* 36 (2): 97–118.

Hellwig, S.J., Monroe, E.E. and Jacobs, J. (2000) Making informed choices: selecting children's trade books for mathematics instruction. *Teaching Children Mathematics Journal,* 7 (3): 138–45.

Kinniburgh, L.H. and Byrd, K. (2008) Ten black dots and September 11: Integrating social studies and mathematics through children's literature. *Social Studies,* 99 (1): 33–36.

Levene, S.C., Suriyakham, L.W., Rowe, M.L., Huttenlocher, J. and Gunderson, E.A. (2010) What counts in the development of young children's number knowledge? *Developmental Psychology,* 46 (5): 1309–1319.

Lucey, T.A. and Maxwell, S.A. (2009) Preservice elementary teachers' confidence in teaching about money. *Curriculum and Teaching Dialogue,* 11, (1 and 2): 221–237.

MacGregor, M. (2002) Using words to explain mathematical ideas. *Australian Journal of Language and Literacy Articles.* Available at **http://www.highbeam.com/doc/1G1-84543400. html** (accessed 16/3/11).

Merenda, R.C. (2000) Numeracy encounters in a book bag: Meeting the NCTM Standards. *Early Childhood Education Journal,* 27 (3): 151–158.

Noss, R. and Hoyles, C. (1996) *Windows on Mathematical Meanings: Learning Cultures and Computers.* Dordrecht: Kluwer Academic Publishers.

Spiering, M. (2001) The imperial system of weights and measures: traditional, superior and banned by Europe? *Contemporary British History,* 15 (4): 111–129.

Tan, K.C. and Chua, B.L. (2006) The sound of music and its link with mathematics. *Teaching Mathematics and its Applications,* 25 (4): 181–188.

Tsao, Y-Ling (2010) Integrating the design mathematical trail in mathematics curriculum for the sixth grade student. *Journal of Instructional Psychology*, 37 (1): 81–96.

Tucker, C., Boggan, M. and Harper, S. (2010) Using children's literature to teach measurement. *Reading Improvement*, 47 (3): 154–161.

Williams, P. (2008) *Independent review of mathematics teaching in early years settings and primary schools. Final report.* London: DCSF.

3. Shape and space

Introduction

Many people perceive mathematics as only arithmetic and as a result they often refer to it as 'sums'. They think mathematics is something they did at school and did not particularly like, and often profess to not being able to 'do' mathematics. However, mathematics is a much wider subject than calculation. This chapter will continue to develop the ideas raised in Chapter 1 with regard to using and applying mathematics, in the context of shape and space. It will look at how use and application of shape and space can be used to develop both mathematical ideas as well as enhance the understanding of other subject areas. However, whether learning or teaching mathematics it is very difficult to separate totally the various different elements involved. Once again we are led into the discussion of integration but this time within mathematics itself. Therefore you need to be aware that while the focus of this chapter is shape and space, the skills required to complete a given problem also sit within the realms of number, measure or data handling or may be all of these combined.

The language of shape

As with all other areas of mathematics the correct language of shape and space needs to be learned and used from the outset in order to cause the least confusion as children develop and begin to apply their understanding to the world around them.

The historical development of naming shapes

In number, the stable-order labels (1, 2, 3 and so on) and our place-value system allow us to create far more numbers than our memories could ever hold. This makes using and applying mathematics involving numbers relatively straightforward. However, this is not the case for shapes. Many of the labels given to figures historically tended to be based on environmental factors or uses and this led to fairly arbitrary labels which reflected no logical sequence. Therefore knowing and using the correct geometric terminology is more difficult than number (Hansen, 2008). For example, the term *isosceles* is used only twice in geometry: to qualify particular types of triangle and trapezium. Its Greek roots refer to the equal (*isos*) legs (*skelos*) of the figures, with two sides the same length. The term *rhombus* is also from Greek, but referred to a toy, a bullroarer, which was spun quickly to make a distinct sound. *Rhomb*, meaning turn, gave the figure its name. To complicate matters further, there is a lack of consistency between how the labels are used in some countries. For example, in the USA *trapezium* is used for quadrilaterals that have no sides parallel, whereas in England (and elsewhere) *trapezoid* is used for this purpose. *Trapezium* in England and elsewhere is a figure having two sides parallel (Usiskin and Griffin, 2008).

> ## Activity
> What do you know about triangles?
> Triangles are named either by their sides (equilateral, isosceles and scalene) or their angles (acute, right, obtuse, equiangular).
> Make a list of the seven types of triangles. Next to them, make a note about your knowledge and understanding of: (a) their angles, (b) their sides, and (c) the etymology (origins) of the word. Can you draw an example of each triangle?

The etymologies of the labels 'equilateral', 'isosceles' and 'scalene' are very interesting. Above the activity you read that *isosceles* has Greek roots. *Scalene* is also from Greek. *Skalenos* means 'hoed up', and later meant 'cut up'. A hoed ground is uneven and of course the sides of a scalene triangle are also uneven. It may surprise you to know that although these other two labels are from Greek origins, *equilateral* is not. Instead it is from the Latin *æquus*, meaning 'even' and *latus* (which subsequently became *later*) meaning side (Schwartzman, 1994).

How familiar were you with the term 'equiangular'? Although it was a term used by Euclid in his *Elements* Book I, equilateral is more commonly used. Of course the label refers to equal angles. It is likely that you were able to make notes about the angles and sides of each of the triangles listed. If you would like more help with that particular task, see the Further Reading section at the end of this chapter.

Later on, there came a more consistent approach to labelling geometric figures to some extent. This developed alongside humankind's understanding for the need of a more logical approach to geometry, including nomenclature and classification. This can be seen, for example, in the naming of 2D figures according to their number of sides and in 3D solids according to their number of faces. Commonly polygons with more than ten sides are often referred to as *n-gon*. For example a tetrakaidecagon is more easily referred to as a 14-gon. For further discussion on the definitions of quadrilaterals, see later in the chapter.

Shape terminology and everyday language

Much of the language used when referring to shape can also be found in everyday language. This can cause confusion because the same word may have a completely different meaning. Children not only need to be aware of these differences but need to be able to select and use the appropriate words in the different situations.

Table 3.1 gives some examples of shape-related words that are also used in everyday contexts.

volume	kite	cone	regular	irregular	segment
rotation	map	degree	chord	face	solid
star	angle	line	similar	surface	round

Table 3.1 Ambiguous terminology

It is particularly important that all aspects of shape are discussed and explored if children are to be able to recognise and use this knowledge effectively both in a mathematical context and in other curriculum subjects. All too often children can be heard using mathematics vocabulary within the allotted mathematics lesson but when completing similar activities in other subjects reverting to more common everyday language (for an example, read the Case Study 'Making links between lessons' in Chapter 1). The result of this is that the children do not connect mathematics with other subjects and teachers miss assessment opportunities (for an example, read the Case Study 'Using assessment evidence from beyond the mathematics lesson' in Chapter 1).

If children are to be confident mathematicians using vocabulary in different contexts then it is essential for you to model the vocabulary that is to be used during the lesson. Additionally, this modelling of language needs to continue throughout the teaching of other subjects. It may well be the case that the same word is used to mean different things during the day and so you will need to help the children learn the skills to be able to recognise the context and therefore meaning in which the word is used.

Activity

The research focus that follows explores the ambiguity of language in mathematics. As you are reading it, think about how you perceive language use. Reflect on your mathematics teaching and to what extent you have thought about language.

Research Focus: Ambiguity in mathematical language

Barwell (2005) identifies two different ways of thinking about language, which he defines as two models: the formal model and the discursive model.

The formal model considers mathematical language as explicit and formal. This model allows no room for mathematical ambiguity because it sees vocabulary as being used to precisely define terms. However, in this model ambiguities are likely to occur between technical and everyday words. Barwell identifies that the National Numeracy Strategy encourages this formal model's thinking about mathematical language: *You need to plan the introduction of new words in a suitable context...Explain their meanings carefully and rehearse them several times...sort out any ambiguities or misconceptions your pupils may have through a range of...questions.* (DfEE, 2000, page 2, cited in Barwell, 2005, page 121).

On the other hand, the discursive model considers mathematical language as a tool for constructing mathematical understanding. This model accepts that defining can occur in a number of ways. In this model, ambiguity is encouraged, as it is seen as a resource for learning mathematics. Barwell (2005, page 124) provides an example of an ambiguity where *a picture of a square is treated as if it is perfectly square for the purposes of mathematical discussion, in the same way that plastic shapes are*

$\longrightarrow$

> to be treated as two dimensional when they can also be seen as three dimensional (Barwell, 2005, page 124).
>
> The two models are not in opposition. After all, it is important that children do learn to use formal mathematical language. Barwell points out that learning formal mathematical language *is not identical with learning mathematical vocabulary. Rather, students' development of the use of mathematical discourse is intertwined with their development of mathematical thinking. Ambiguity acts as an important resource for students and teachers, serving as a means of articulating between thinking and discourse* (page 125). (You can read about this in practice in the case study 'Distinguishing between 2D and 3D shapes' in the next section.)

Now that we have outlined a little of the history and the complexities of the language of shape we turn our attention to how this translates into practice, how important it is to ensure that children are not misled or confused by teaching methods used, and how by listening to children's responses you too can learn from them.

2D and 3D shape and space

Thinking about shape and space according to dimensions

Although we most commonly talk about two and three dimensions in Key Stages 1 and 2, when you are thinking about shape and space (often the full title of this programme of study is overlooked) you should actually be aware of more dimensions. Let's start with two dimensions. We know that a polygon is created on a plane, a 2D region that is bound by three or more lines or line segments. In three dimensions, these polygons become faces if they encapsulate a space. The space inside the faces is referred to as the volume. Further in this chapter and in Chapter 4 you will be encouraged to think more about teaching and learning using these terms. So, we have looked at 3D and 2D. Let's keep working back. When there is one dimension, a line, line segment or edge are identified. When there are zero dimensions, we find a point or a vertex. Do you think we can extend the pattern in both directions? Well, abstract mathematicians and scientists do. They work with the null polytype which is found in −1 dimension and the spacetime continuum which operates with a fourth dimension. Dimensions are important in measurement as well as shape and space, and you will read more about dimensions in Chapter 4.

Exploring 2D and 3D shape and space with children

There is much discussion regarding how and when children should be introduced to 2D and 3D shape and space. One argument is to introduce 2D first, another suggests that 3D should come first and yet another would argue that they should be taught together (for example, see how Roth and Thom (2009) and Tsao (2010) explore the relationship between 2D and 3D shape). We live in a three-dimensional world and if children are to make sense of this world in terms of what they learn then perhaps the argument for teaching 3D followed by 2D might have some credence. As discussed above, the major problems to try to overcome when teaching this part of shape are to ensure that the true sense of dimension is understood, and to check that children are not given false information regarding 2D shape. As you read the case study below, think carefully of your own experiences of teaching and learning shape and space.

Case Study: Distinguishing between 2D and 3D shapes

Barry is a trainee teacher on his penultimate placement in a Year 1 class. He is keen for the children to be able to recognise shapes and the corresponding name for these shapes. He decides that a practical activity would probably be best and sets about making resources so that he is fully prepared for the lesson. Throughout his study of English modules it has been stressed how important it is to use appropriate fonts when preparing resources for school. This is mainly due to the huge emphasis on phonics and word recognition but he recalls that it has also been mentioned in mathematics modules in terms of numbers.

All begins well as Barry uses a prepared flipchart with 2D shapes clearly drawn and individual shape names on laminated card ready for the children to stick on to the correct shape. The children are keen to show what they know and are more than able to identify the figures as Barry reads out the name.

Once all the children have successfully named a shape, Barry divides the class into two groups and hands out the laminated shape names to the children in one group. To the other half he hands out plastic shapes and explains that for this activity the children will need to find their partner by matching the name to the shape. One child, Fiona, is a little confused. During the starter activity Barry had said more than once that he had drawn the shapes onto the flipchart as today they were talking about 2D shape. These, he had pointed out, were flat shapes that you couldn't pick up. Fiona looks at the shape she has been given and reasons that it must be 3D as she is holding the shape in her hand. She questions Barry about this and he explains that the shapes they are using are very thin so they are almost 2D. Confused, but seemingly satisfied with this explanation, she goes to try and find her partner.

The other children begin to look for their partners, by comparing names to shapes and once they have achieved this they sit down on the carpet together ready to show each other. It is during this activity that four children begin to have an argument and the tears begin to flow. Barry notices and asks the children to explain what the problem is.

Sam: I have the word rectangle and Jo is holding a square but says he is my partner.

→

Jo: I *am* his partner because a square *is* a rectangle.

Ciara: No it's not! I have the word square and so *I* should be Jo's partner.

Neil: And I have the rectangle shape so I can't be Ciara's partner because a rectangle isn't a square.

Barry listens to the children and agrees with Jo that she is absolutely correct and that a square is indeed an example of rectangle. By now other children have started to join in the discussion and Fiona is still not really sure about the shape she is holding being 2D. Barry chooses to stop the activity at this point, bring the children together and try to address these two issues.

Links to the National Curriculum

While the lesson in the case study above has the mathematical focus of shape recognition (Ma3 2b: describe common 2D shapes; name and describe the mathematical features of common 2D shapes, including triangles of various kinds, rectangles including squares, circles, hexagons, pentagons), there is also the opportunity for children to practise word recognition and graphic knowledge (En2 1f, g).

Activity

What do you think was the main problem in this lesson?
How could Barry have avoided the two issues raised?
Do you think Barry has a clear understanding of the properties of shapes?

Imagine you are Barry and think what you would now say to the children in order to:

• correct the mistake of using 3D shapes and calling them 2D;
• explain how a square is a rectangle.

Although Barry had planned and prepared his lesson well in advance, he only realised his errors when they were pointed out to him by Fiona and Jo. It is essential that you are familiar with the properties of shapes and the associated vocabulary, but this case study also clearly identifies the need for you to realise that much of what you will learn as you train will come directly from the children.

When questioning it is vital that you really do listen to the answers the children give. Like Barry you need to respond in a way that is not dismissive to the child, but at the same time does not reinforce misconceptions that you later have to rectify. Telling Fiona that the shape was 'nearly 2D' only created more confusion and the need for further explanation later.

In Chapter 2 we discussed the potential confusion with the use of 'couple', which is another example of children assimilating given information only to be confused by the teacher's delivery of these words. Within a dedicated mathematics lesson it is common practice to use different terminology in order that children do not rely on just one word. For example, addition, increase, plus, and more than, can all refer to the same function. In the same way words related to shape can refer to the same shape. A square could be referred to as a square, rectangle, rhombus, parallelogram, and kite.

Thinking about squares and rectangles

In the activity above you were asked to think about Barry's situation regarding the children's confusion between the terms *square* and *rectangle*.

Table 3.2 shows how the properties of quadrilaterals also satisfy the definition of a square. Although is it unlikely that you would explore the properties in exactly this way with children of the age in the case study, you could use some of the information in the table yourself to help children to understand how a square can be an example of many different definitions of figures. We know that figures can be defined in many different ways (such as using sides, angles, symmetries, diagonals). The table develops only sides and angles in different types of quadrilaterals in order for you and the children to see that a square can be a particular instantiation of all the definitions in the table.

A square has the following properties ...	So does a ...	So a square is also a ...
Four sides	Quadrilateral	Quadrilateral
Four sides (and) At least one pair of parallel sides	Quadrilateral Trapezium	Quadrilateral Trapezium
Exactly two pairs of equal length adjacent sides	Quadrilateral Kite	Quadrilateral Kite
Exactly two pairs of parallel sides Exactly two pairs of equal opposite sides Exactly two pairs of equal opposite angles	Quadrilateral Parallelogram	Quadrilateral Parallelogram
Exactly two pairs of parallel sides Exactly two pairs of equal opposite sides All interior angles are equal (all right angles)	Quadrilateral Parallelogram Rectangle (meaning right angle)	Quadrilateral Parallelogram Rectangle (meaning right angle)
Exactly two pairs of parallel sides Exactly two pairs of equal opposite angles Four sides are equal length.	Quadrilateral Parallelogram Rhombus	Quadrilateral Parallelogram Rhombus
Exactly two pairs of parallel sides Four sides are equal length All interior angles are equal (all right angles)	Quadrilateral Trapezium Kite Parallelogram Rhombus Rectangle	Quadrilateral Trapezium Kite Parallelogram Rhombus Rectangle

Table 3.2 Properties of quadrilaterals

In many primary classrooms we have witnessed the technical language of the English curriculum (such as genre and imperative verbs) being used confidently by children as young as six years of age. We would like to be able to see similarities with this for mathematics language. Just as was the case in English, there is a need for mathematical language to be modelled by teachers and used by children within other subjects to describe actions and tasks if there is going to be any chance of mathematical vocabulary being integrated into common language acquisition. An example of this integration of language was witnessed in a Year 1 class where a trainee teacher was recapping a story during a literacy lesson. As the children recounted the story they were encouraged to use words such as 'sequence' and 'order'. When describing items in the story they were encouraged to compare size and list things in ascending order.

The following section explores two more areas of mathematics where the need to use the correct terminology is once again highlighted – congruence and similarity.

Congruence and similarity

How familiar are you with these two words? You probably use the word 'similar' but how often would you use the word 'congruent'? Having said this, in what way do you use the word 'similar'? If we think of the statement: *My house is very similar to yours,* what does it actually mean? You may think it means that one house is very like another. It may have the same layout of rooms, etc., but in mathematics the term 'similar' when used in the context of shape means an identical shape, just a different size. In Key Stage 2 it is often called enlargement. 'Congruency' is the term used to describe shapes that are exactly the same. They could, however, be in different orientations or flipped. Both terms are more likely to be used in Key Stage 2, but some Key Stage 1 children may be able to use them confidently. As with all teaching, you need to think of the children's attainment when planning rather than the year group they happen to be in.

Case Study: Maths from different cultures

Georgia is a trainee teacher on placement in a year 4 class. The children have recently been involved in a local village agricultural show where they all had to produce a piece of craft work and she had chosen for them to create origami flowers. During the preparation for the show one of the children had opened up the finished flower and had been fascinated by the shapes that the folding had produced. Georgia decided to look further at paper folding and in particular the origins and construction of tangrams. As part of a wider theme, the children began their investigation with a study of China and the meaning of the word 'Origami' before going on to create their own tangram.

$\rightarrow$

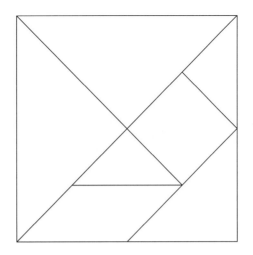

Figure 3.1 Tangram

Georgia showed the children a wooden tangram (Figure 3.1) and then explained that it was possible to fold a square of paper to form the shapes they could see. Once all the children had been successful at this they were then asked to work together to explore the shapes they had made and describe them to a partner. They began by giving the shapes names such as triangle and square and were quickly able to establish that they had five triangles, one square and one parallelogram. The children then moved on to the computers where a prepared tangram had been provided for them so that they could manipulate the 2D shapes and investigate the size, area, proportion, etc. Georgia asked them to record their findings ready to share with the rest of the class. One child, Sarah explained the following to Georgia.

S: There are two large triangles that are exactly the same.

G: Do you know what we call that?

S: No.

G: We say they are *congruent*, which means exactly the same.

S: OK...anyway the two small triangles are the same too. Sorry congruent. But if you look at them they look the same as the large ones, just smaller.

G: You're absolutely right, Sarah, and there is a name for that too.

S: Thought there might be!

G: Ha ha...well we call those shapes *similar* because, just as you said, they have the same size angles, but the sides are different lengths.

S: The middle sized triangle is on its own though.

G: That's right but if you turn it round and look closely, what do you notice?

S: Oh yes, look it is similar because it's bigger than the small ones but not as big as the large one.

Georgia then shows Sarah that she can place the triangles on top of one another to show that the angles are the same and it is the length of the sides that are different. The children go on to discover that by using the knowledge of the size of the triangles they can explain the size of the square and parallelogram in terms of their area, how many triangles they can fit into them, and begin to use the language of fractions in their recordings as shown in Table 3.3.

Large triangle	Congruent with other large triangle. Similar to large/small triangles. Quarter of the area of the whole original square. Twice the area of the medium triangle. Four times the area of the small triangle.
Medium triangle	Similar to large/small triangles. Half the area of large triangle. Twice the area of the small triangle. One-eighth of the area of the original large square.
Small triangle	Similar to the large/medium triangles. Half the area of the square. Half the area of the parallelogram. Half the area of the medium triangle. One-quarter the area of the large triangle. One-sixteenth the area of the large square.
Square	Twice the area of the small triangle. Equal to the area of the parallelogram. Equal to the area of the medium triangle. One-eighth of the area of the original large square.
Parallelogram	Twice the area of the small triangle. Equal to the area of the square and medium triangle. One-eighth of the area of the original large square.

Table 3.3 Relationships in the tangram

Georgia was able to observe and listen to the children as they discussed what they had found, and was then able to use this information to plan and develop lessons involving area. She was impressed by the children's ability to be able to reason and problem-solve, not only while folding the paper but also when comparing the shapes.

Links to the National Curriculum

Many of the mathematics programmes of study related to shape and space (Ma3) are clearly recognisable from the above case study such as:

- describe 2D shapes and the way they behave, making more precise use of geometrical language (2b);

> ● transform objects in practical situations, transform images using ICT (3b).
>
> However, by combining this activity with learning about China and the origins of origami, Georgia was also able to involve children in locating and describing places which forms part of the geography programme of study (3b, 3c). Some of the children also used ICT which helped children to manipulate the shapes and identify patterns and relationships (2c).

The case study above and thinking about properties of quadrilaterals in relation to a square earlier in the chapter have helped to highlight the need to encourage children to compare and contrast shapes and recognise the similarities and differences. The tangram activity in particular introduces the idea of conservation of area which will be discussed in more detail in Chapter 4. In the next section we show how area and perimeter in the mathematics curriculum can be taught in a practical and cross-curricular way.

Area and perimeter

Too often we see children being required to calculate the area or perimeter of shapes by looking at the numeric values of the lengths of the sides and perform an algorithm (such as area for a rectangle or parallelogram = base × height). The problems become less to do with area and perimeter and more to do with multiplication and addition. When this is done, the shape and space element has been sidelined. The case study below outlines how one trainee uses a real problem and follows it through from the planning stage to an end product, with the children using practical application of their knowledge and skills.

Case Study: A new school garden

Daniel is a trainee teacher on placement in a Year 5 class. He has been told that the children are struggling to understand area and perimeter and that they are confusing the two.

The class he is working in includes one child, Zoe, whose father is the manager of a large DIY store. He has offered to make quite a substantial gift to the school as all four of his children have attended and he wants to show his appreciation. After much discussion between the head teacher and Zoe's dad it is decided to create a garden for the school within the existing grounds. Daniel and the class teacher work together to plan a series of lessons to get the children involved in the practical application of area and perimeter and in turn produce a plan for the new garden. Daniel has struggled himself in the past with remembering what these terms mean and is keen to explain that the way he remembers the difference is by thinking of area as 'arena' and perimeter as 'meter.' This way when he thinks about them he thinks of an arena as inside at a concert and meter as a length. The children think this is a good idea and can be heard later in the week reminding each other using Daniel's advice.

→

Zoe's father provides a list of all the things that the store will provide in order for a garden to be created at the school. He explains that he will also provide the labour to carry out the ground work and the initial planting. It will then be the children's responsibility to continue to take care of the garden.

The governors are more than delighted at this generous offer and meet with the children to decide what should be included in the garden. They go through the list from Zoe's dad and after much lively discussion the children have enough information to prepare their plans for submission to the governors and the choice of garden design to be made. The children are really excited to begin so Daniel takes them out on to the field and shows them the site of the new garden, reinforcing the perimeter and area of the space they have. Some children go straight to the computer, others prefer to create a rough sketch of the ideas first, while others decide to create scaled-down cardboard cut-outs of all the items and begin to manipulate them to fit into the given space.

Through discussion and collaboration all the children are able to create different garden designs that include accurate perimeter and area measurements and good reasons for their choices. These are then presented to the governing body and one is selected.

The children's designs are used to create a display in the school and it is not long before a large lorry arrives at the school with all that is needed to create the new garden. To the children's delight, Zoe's father is on the lorry, along with several other members of staff from the DIY store. The designated part of the field is transformed into a garden for the whole school to use and photos are taken of the work as it progresses and these are added to the display in school.

Governors and parents are invited to the opening and Zoe is given the honour of being the first person to walk through the garden.

Links to the National Curriculum

By combining skills involved in design and technology with mathematics in this way children were able to reflect on their work as they designed and made it, identifying improvements (D&T 3a), selecting appropriate tools and techniques (D&T 2a) and measuring, marking out, cutting and shaping a range of materials (D&T 2d). They were also able to extend their knowledge of area and perimeter beyond finding and calculating perimeters and areas of simple shapes (Ma1 4e).

In the above case study the children had a purpose for the work they were being asked to do. There was a starting point and a product at the end. In this case, the children were required to use and apply their knowledge of area and perimeter to achieve the desired results. All too often mathematics is seen as a paper exercise with no real purpose other than to find an answer. It is not in every school that you will have such an opportunity to create a garden but there is much of the curriculum that can be approached in the same way as Daniel and his class teacher did with the garden.

Never underestimate the sheer diverse nature of experience and interest among the children, parents/carers, grandparents, etc. For example, we have seen a class of Year 6 trying to get to grips with a technology project involving cams only to be interrupted one afternoon by one of the parents bringing in a car engine. One child in the class had mentioned what they were doing so the parent thought they might like a real example. Many schools have very talented parents able to write music, sing, dance, recite, etc., and in some schools all these things are combined to produce noteworthy school productions. The opportunities to develop mathematics in such projects are endless.

Co-ordinates and direction

When learning about the skills associated with co-ordinates and graphs you will often hear teachers tell children that *you go along the corridor and up the stairs* in order to remember the order of the (x,y) co-ordinates when plotting points on a grid. While this is a useful *aide-mémoire* for reading maps, there are many ways that co-ordinates and direction can be incorporated into other subjects. With the increasing accessibility of technology within schools, children need to become proficient at understanding and applying the skills and language of co-ordination and direction. From Key Stage 1 children are expected to be able to begin to programme floor turtles to complete simple courses. In Key Stage 2 children write simple computer programs, read maps and use grid references more accurately. Many schools now regularly make use of internet downloads such as Google Earth to study different locations, and so children need to quickly become familiar with the many functions and capabilities of such resources. This move towards a more technological learning environment brings the world around us into the classroom and children are able to see and experience the links between the different subjects first hand.

Links to the National Curriculum
The following list shows how there are a significant number of objectives that relate to direction and co-ordinates across a number of subjects.

Mathematics: Understanding properties of position and movement (Ma3)
Key Stage 1: observe, visualise and describe positions, directions and movements using common words (3a);
recognise movements in a straight line and rotations and combine them in simple ways (3b);
recognise right angles (3c).

Key Stage 2: visualise and describe movements using appropriate language (3a); transform objects in practical situations; transform images using ICT; visualise and predict the position of a shape following a rotation, reflection or translation (3b); identify and draw 2D shapes in different orientations on grids; locate and draw shapes using coordinates in the first quadrant, then all four (3c).

ICT: Developing ideas and making things happen.
Key Stage 1: plan and give instructions to make things happen (2c).
Key Stage 2: create, test, improve and refine sequences of instructions to make things happen and to monitor and respond to them (2b).

Geography: Geographical enquiry
Key Stage 1: use globes, maps and plans at a range of scales (2c).
Key Stage 2: use atlases and globes, and maps and plans at a range of scales (2c).

PE: Dance
Key Stage 1: use movement imaginatively, responding to stimuli (6a); change the rhythm, speed, level and direction of their movements (6b).
Key Stage 2: create and perform dances using a range of movement patterns (6a).

Games activities
Key Stage 1: travel with, send and receive a ball and other equipment in different ways (7a).

Science: Forces and motion (Sc 4)
Key Stage 1: find more about, and describe the movement of familiar things (2a).
Key Stage 2: the forces of attraction and repulsion between magnets and materials (2a); objects are pulled downwards because of the gravitational attraction between them and the earth (2b); friction, air resistance as a force slows moving objects and may prevent them from starting to move (2c).

The chapter so far has concentrated mostly on 2D shape and the importance of children's understanding of dimension. We move now to consider three-dimensional space and how this can be taught in a way that is meaningful and relevant to children. There is an expectation and requirement in the National Curriculum that children should be able to recognise a 3D shape from a 2D net. Time is spent in schools drawing all the nets of a cube and then folding them carefully until all the different configuration of six squares has been drawn, cut out and folded.

In Chapter 2 stories were given as an effective way to teach mathematics across the curriculum. The research focus below explores how stories can be used to explore geometrical concepts.

Research Focus: Story bags

Merenda (2000) looked at the use of story bags in a US home–school project that involved first-grade children and their parents in undertaking mathematics activities based on the book *Ten black dots* by Donald Crews which looks at shape. Story bags are designed by teachers to include games and activities related to a book. The bags are designed to be enjoyed at home and brought back to the nursery or school to swap with another. Merenda explains how the story bags enable the children to *engage in problem solving, communication, reasoning, connections, number sense and numeration* (page 151). This particular book also encouraged the children to produce their own creative responses to a geometric problem set. The children and parents shared mathematics ideas verbally and represented those ideas symbolically.

Also using a geometry context, Capraro and Capraro's (2006) research shows us that using story should not be limited to younger learners. In their article, they identify the influence of language on mathematical attainment, noting that communication and contexts that are real to the children are key to their learning. In their research, Capraro and Capraro set out to explore the extent to which books could improve middle-school children's sense-making of mathematical vocabulary. Using a mixed-methods approach, they worked with 105 Year 6 children, some of whom had the literature intervention (being read *Sir Cumference and the Dragon of Pi*) and some who did not. Capraro and Capraro explain how the lessons integrated literature, geometry, measurement, fractions, and division, with the teacher focusing on developing geometry vocabulary and concepts.

Their findings identified that the children who had been read to had a statistically significant improvement on both the topic and mathematics generally, which they believe occurred because the children were able to develop formulae and procedures that were meaningful to them, rather than by rote learning. There was no difference between the two groups on general reading, even though the book held the attention and interest of the children.

The case study that follows shows how Jennifer used her own version of a traditional story to teach elements of 3D shape.

Case Study: Philip's house

Jennifer was an English specialist on her final placement in a Reception to Year 2 class and she was very keen to develop the idea of using stories to enhance

→

learning. Part of one of her assignments had been to review traditional stories and the underlying messages they gave to children. She had been intrigued that many depicted animals as people and were quite violent, so she decided to rewrite some of them to still retain the concept of the story but using real people and depicting the violence in an alternative way. She then tweaked one of the stories further to use in the teaching of 3D shape.

Jennifer began by reading the story to the children:

Philip's House

It was a few days before the beginning of the long summer holidays and mum was remembering last year when the triplets had made so much mess in the house. This year she had a plan.

When the boys came in from school she sat them down and asked them if they would like to spend the holidays building a play house in the garden. They thought this was an excellent idea and were really excited to begin, but although they looked alike they were very different in lots of other ways.

Peter was always rushing around trying to get things finished as quickly as possible. Paul always started off with good intentions but gave up soon after he had started and rushed things to get them finished. Philip always read instructions, took his time and saw things through to the finish. As you can imagine, when they sat down to discuss the house they were going to build they soon fell out.

Mum suggested that they build a house each and then decide whose was the best. The boys agreed but wanted to know who would decide. Mum thought for a moment and then told them that as the house would have to be left in the garden it would need to stand up to the strong winds that were forecast at the end of the summer, so they would let the wind decide which house was the best.

The triplets' dad owned a building firm and mum ran a busy stables so there were many things to choose from to build their houses. Peter decided that he would use some straw and some string. Paul decided that he would use some wood and some glue. Philip decided that he would use some bricks, some wood and some cement. They all collected what they needed and began to build.

*Peter took the straw and tied it together in bundles to build something that looked like a **cone or a triangular prism**. He didn't mind that it was a bit wobbly, he was glad he had finished. He stood back to admire what he had built and began to fill his house with toys. Paul took a little longer. At first he carefully measured all the wood and cut it to the correct length, but he soon became bored with this and wanted to play like Peter. He quickly finished his house and stood back to admire what he had built. **It looked a bit like a cuboid but had bits missing**. There were no*

→

end **faces** so it was more like a tunnel. He wasn't really bothered though and began to fill his house with toys.

All this time Philip had been busy drawing plans for his house and collecting all the extra bits and pieces he would need. Only when he had checked and double checked did he begin to build his house. It took him so long that the holiday was almost over. He did have time to stand back and admire his house though. What he saw was **a solid cuboid with six faces. On top was a sturdy triangular prism roof with a firm base fixed to the cuboid with cement.**

Just then the wind began to blow hard, he had no time to fill his house with toys before the weather began to change and the wind continued to blow. The three boys ran into their houses and closed the doors.

The wind blew and blew. At first nothing happened. Then bit by bit Peter's straw house began to fly away. He had forgotten to give it a **base** and so the **sides** simply collapsed. The wind blew and blew until suddenly his whole house flew across the garden and landed in a heap. He quickly gathered up his toys and ran to Paul's house. Paul let him in, but was not very happy himself as his house was starting to rattle and shake. The open ends let the wind whistle through the tunnel.

The wind blew and blew. Bit by bit Paul's wooden house began to fly away. The wind blew and blew until suddenly his whole house flew across the garden and landed in a heap on top of the straw. They both grabbed their toys and ran to Philip's house.

Philip let them in and although he didn't like the noise of the wind blowing down the chimney he was quite calm. He shut the door tight and they began to play with the toys they had rescued. The wind still blew and blew, but Philip's house was strong and never blew away. In fact it was so well built that from that summer on the boys had many great adventures in Philip's house.

After the children had heard this story they were able to begin to construct their own houses and test the strength of different shapes using a hairdryer. They went on to look at different shapes involved in the construction of the school, such as rectangular windows, doors, etc. They also examined the play house to discover the shapes that it was made from. Eventually this lead to investigation of 3D cardboard boxes to observe the different nets and much problem solving, reasoning and communication to discover the strongest shape.

Once all the construction work had finished and children had successfully made their own houses they were able to recreate and perform the story in assembly for the rest of the school.

Links to the National Curriculum

Having made their houses, the children were able to recreate the effects of the wind to test the strength of their structure. This increased their knowledge and understanding of pattern processes, materials and components and patterns and properties of shape. In doing so the following areas were addressed.

Mathematics: understanding patterns and properties of shape (Ma3);
describe properties of shapes that they can see or visualise using related vocabulary (2a);
observe, handle and describe common 2D and 3D shapes; name and describe the mathematical features of common 2D and 3D shapes, including triangles of various kinds, rectangles including squares, circles, cubes, cuboids (2b);
create 3D shapes (2c).

Geography: knowledge and understanding of pattern and processes;
recognise changes in physical features (4b).

Design and technology: knowledge and understanding of materials and components;
the working characteristics of materials (4a).

Performing their version of the story in assembly, the children were able to use language and actions to explore and convey situations, characters and emotions (En14a) and create and sustain roles individually and when working with others (4b).

Learning Outcomes Review

This chapter has explored the origins of shape names, describing how there is no real pattern or logic to these labels. This leads to the ambiguity of the language, particularly in the case of 2D and 3D shape and the recognition of the need to avoid giving children incorrect information. The chapter describes practical ways of teaching congruence, similarity, area and perimeter before finishing with a return to the idea of teaching through story to create 3D shapes.

Self-assessment questions

1. Continue to make a bank of words that are ambiguous. Include the mathematical and everyday definitions.
2. Create an inclusive definition of a square using its symmetry properties.
3. Define *congruent* and *similar*.
4. Define *area* and *perimeter*.

Further Reading

Hansen, A. (2008) *Primary mathematics: Extending knowledge in practice*. Exeter: Learning Matters. Chapter 5 discusses the classification of triangles, using the lengths of sides or the size of their angles.

Hansen, A. (2011) *Children's errors in mathematics*. Exeter: Learning Matters. Chapter 1 considers the complexity of defining quadrilaterals in further depth.

References

Barwell, R. (2005) Ambiguity in the mathematics classroom. *Language and Education*, 19 (2): 118–126.

Capraro, R.M. and Capraro, M.M. (2006) Are you really going to read us a story? Learning geometry through children's mathematics literature. *Reading Psychology*, 24: 21–36.

Hansen, A. (2008) *Children's geometric defining and a principled approach to task design*. Unpublished doctoral thesis. Institute of Education, University of Warwick. Available at **www.children-count.co.uk/images/Phd%20final.pdf**

Merenda, R.C. (2000) Numeracy encounters in a book bag: meeting the NCTM standards. *Early Childhood Education Journal*, 27(3): 151–157.

Roth, W-M. and Thom, J. S (2009) The emergence of 3D geometry from children's (teacher-guided) classification tasks. *The Journal of the Learning Sciences*, 18: 45–99.

Schwartzman, S. (1994) *The words of mathematics: An etymological dictionary of mathematical terms used in English*. Washington, DC: The Mathematical Association of America.

Tsao, Y-L. (2010) Integrating the design mathematical trail in mathematics curriculum for the sixth grade student. *Journal of Instructional Psychology*, 37 (1): 81–96.

Usiskin, Z. and Griffin, J. (2008) *The classification of quadrilaterals: A study of definition*. Charlotte, NC: Information Age Publishing Inc.

4. Measures

Introduction

This chapter, like the others before it, explores how measurement can be used as a tool to learn other curriculum subjects, as well as how other subjects can be used to develop children's understanding of measures.

When thinking about measures in a cross-curricular, practical and meaningful way, it is almost impossible to focus on only one aspect of measurement because they are all very much interrelated, as this chapter will show. For example, when cooking, it could be possible to use and apply knowledge, skills and understanding about length and area when lining a tin; mass and capacity when measuring ingredients and choosing an appropriate tin; as well as temperature and time when baking the cake. Therefore, we advise you to scan this whole chapter, or use the index, to find discussion about any particular aspects of measurement you are focusing on at this stage, rather than simply go to one section that might have the title of what you are looking for.

This chapter begins by exploring the importance of transitivity, conservation and *estimation* and how language and practical experience of measures are essential to develop these notions. The chapter goes on to discuss various content of the National Curriculum: length and area, angle, time, volume and capacity, and mass. The chapter concludes with an example of how the skill of reading scales can be used across a number of measurement units to develop children's understanding of measurement and its use and application in other subjects.

Estimation

Siegler and Booth (2004, page 428) identify how important estimation is in the lives of adults and children. They provide as examples: *How much time will it take to get home? How much money will the food in the grocery cart cost? How heavy is this object? How far is the distance between here and there? How many weeks will it take to write this paper?* They go on to explain how estimation uses a number of quantitative processes; for example, knowledge of measurement units such as miles, minutes or pounds is required when looking at estimating distance, time or cost.

When estimation skills are used during calculation, it is possible (although not desirable) to be able to estimate in an abstract way. For example, it may be possible for a child to estimate that 27 million add 44 million is around 70 million, without knowing much about 'millions'. However, in measurement, it is very difficult for children to use estimation without having a good understanding of the units being used to measure.

Activity
Think about the following list of units. Note down two or three items that you could measure using each unit.

1. millimetres
2. grams
3. cubic metres
4. pints
5. tonnes
6. hundredths of seconds

7. cup
8. century
9. cm^2
10. decibels

We suspect you found this fairly straightforward. Now, estimate how many units each item on the list would measure. Where possible, check some of your estimations by using a ruler, scales, etc.

Reflect on which of these you found more difficult to estimate and order the units from easiest to most difficult. How does the order of difficulty relate to your experience of using and applying these units?

We suspect that you identified items such as 'beer' and 'milk' that are measured in pints, and that you were able to estimate the number of pints in the objects very easily. We also suspect that you may have found decibels more difficult. Although you may have known what decibels measure, the extent to which you have experienced measuring in decibels is likely to have had an impact on your estimation skills. Andreou and Kotsis (2005) carried out research to explore the ability of blind and sighted children to estimate. They found that children with a visual impairment were better able to estimate, because of the measurement that they carried out in their everyday surroundings which they required in order to have the most control over their lives.

Conservation

Research Focus: Conservation of amount

In 1974 Piaget and Inhelder published a seminal text about children's ability to conserve amounts such as sets of items, mass and volume. The notion of conservation is directly related to one of the core components of this book, reasoning. Piaget's stage theory identified four stages that children move through in their cognitive development. These are the sensorimotor stage, the preoperational stage, the concrete operations stage and the formal operations stage. Part of the theory states that children have reached the concrete operation stage when they are able to conserve in all amounts (Babai, 2009).

Piaget and Inhelder identified the following development of children's understanding of mass, weight, volume and density, which they mapped against the stages of development.

- First, children develop a concept about 'size' in which there is no distinction between mass, weight, volume and density.

→

- Second, during the concrete operations stage, a distinction is made between mass and weight, and the two can be conserved. The concept of 'density' is developed, and differs from their concept of 'weight'.

- Third, during the transition from concrete to formal operation stages, volume is conserved, and is differentiated from mass and weight.

- Finally, in the formal operation stage, because volume and density are consistently differentiated, children's concept of 'density' is identified as a ratio of weight:volume.

(Adapted from Babai, 2009)

Babai (2009) considered a number of test items that asked children about their ability to conserve various mathematical units. Babai found that when children used intuitive reasoning, they often answered conservation questions incorrectly. Those who were able to reason more logically, either visually or linguistically, were more likely to answer the questions correctly. Babai identifies that the higher a child's cognitive level, the more outcomes improved.

What is unclear from Babai's research above is the extent to which the ability to reason is indeed driven by children's stage of development according to Piaget, or whether experience provides opportunity for children to achieve reasoning at an earlier age. Along with others (e.g. Ramos-Christian *et al.*, 2008), we would argue that the latter is an important pedagogical consideration.

Transitive reasoning

Piaget was also the theorist to introduce transitivity. He identified how most children by the age of eight were able to consistently demonstrate transitivity. Research by Long and Kamii (2001) concurs to a certain extent. For example, they found that most children reasoned transitively by Grade 2. The exception to this was the conservation of speed, which was not demonstrated by most until Grade 6. The questions in the activity below come from the level 3–5 2009 Mathematics SATs Test A paper (QCDA, 2009). It is an example of where number and using logical thinking and the notion of transitivity come together.

Activity

As you work though the questions using the information provided, also consider how you would define transitive reasoning.

One battery weighs the same as 60 paperclips.
One pencil sharpener weighs the same as 20 paperclips.

1. How many pencil sharpeners weigh the same as one battery?
2. How many paperclips weigh the same as 2 batteries and 4 pencil sharpeners together?

What is transitivity?

Wright *et al.* (2011, page 57) state that *transitive inference underpins human reasoning competencies,* which they define (page 58) as: *a child is said to possess transitive reasoning when he or she can deduce a latent relationship between two items (say A and C), after being given information about the relationship of each of these items to a third item (B) that just happens to be intermediate between the other two in some respect.* They go on to provide an example of how, later in geometry, it is necessary to perform measurement operations that require transitive deduction.

Although transitive deduction can be carried out using non-standard measures, such as those in the SATs question in the activity above, most mathematics work in school and beyond uses standardised measures.

Why do we need standardised measures?

Units of measurement were among the earliest mathematical tools to be developed by humankind. They were needed to ensure that food or materials were traded fairly and that homes and clothing were measured to ensure effective construction.

The notion of a physical dimension of a quantity was identified by the French mathematician Joseph Fourier (1822), and this notion developed into the SI system, the International System of Units. There are currently seven base quantities that are on the SI system and these have been adopted by most of the countries in the world (with the main exceptions being the USA, Burma and Liberia). The units normally used in primary education are length (SI base unit: metre), time (SI base unit: second) and mass (SI base unit: kilogram). In addition to these there is electric current (SI base unit: ampere), thermodynamic temperature (kelvin), substance (mole) and luminous intensity (candela). As with all mathematics, there are discussions about this being revised, with one suggestion including measuring energy, work and amount of heat (joule), power (watt) and frequency (hertz) (Frantsuz, 2010).

Having a standardised system makes it easier for countries to collaborate and trade. Sometimes not having a standardised system can lead to catastrophic mistakes. For example, in 1999 a NASA spacecraft designed to orbit Mars missed the planet and may now be orbiting the Sun because of a mismatch of the units of measurement being used by engineers on the team based in England and the USA (CNN, 1999). There has been a recent call for NASA to convert its operation to metric in order to support efforts to develop a globalised private space industry. However, NASA has stated that the cost of doing this ($370 million) is too high (New Scientist, 2009).

Links to the National Curriculum
In the mathematics programme of study for measures, the Key Stage 1 objective is to measure objects using uniform non-standard units, then with a standard unit of

length (Ma3 4a). This is extended in Key Stage 2, with children being required to understand the need for standard units of measurement (Ma3 1a, 4a) and choose which ones are suitable for a task, using them to make sensible estimates in everyday situations (Ma3 4a).

Before we look at the content areas of measurement, let us revisit the notion of communication and how having a focus on vocabulary and modelling is a significant factor in being able to develop children's mathematical understanding, this time around using units of measurement.

Communicating measures

In this section we explore how one pedagogical approach involving modern foreign languages (MFL) can support children's understanding of measurement.

Research Focus: Content and Languages Integrated Learning

Content and Languages Integrated Learning (CLIL) is a teaching approach where new ideas and concepts in one subject are taught through a foreign language. Originally an approach used in secondary schools with training CLIL teachers, it is gaining in popularity in primary schools, particularly among those where the primary schoolteacher is a speaker of a foreign language.

One advantage of the CLIL approach is that there is no hard-and-fast rule about how to approach teaching. In fact, Grin (2005) identified 216 different types of CLIL programmes. Philip Hood (online) from the University of Nottingham is a leader in primary CLIL. He identifies four stages of CLIL.

1. *Surface linking.* This is something many MFL teachers do already, for example a short and simple mathematics task in the foreign language. Hood warns that although this is a good starting point, it cannot be considered to be CLIL.

2. *Build new material on to what is already known.* For example, taking an objective learnt the previous year first and then over a series of lessons building on this to teach new objectives.

3. *Teach a completely new topic* in the foreign language.

4. *Partial or full immersion.* This is currently rare in the UK, with only one fully evaluated programme in existence (see Further Reading section).

Hood suggests that a good starting point for teachers is the oral/mental starter in mathematics lessons, *where careful choice of calculations supported by numbers written on the whiteboard, for example division sums [sic] which result in lower*

$\rightarrow$

*number answers or multiplication sums [sic] where one of the multipliers is
gapped, can give both skills practice and a chance to hear higher numbers spoken
by the teacher in a meaningful context* (Hood, online).

Coyle (2007), also at the University of Nottingham, presents a model which
considers the demands placed on learners in four different quadrants (Figure 4.1).
We have adapted the model to pertain to mathematics.

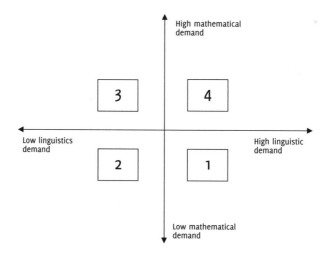

Figure 4.1 The CLIL mathematics matrix (adapted from Coyle, 2007)

*Where the language level of learners is lower than their [mathematics
attainment] level, the learning environment must take into account this
mismatch through ensuring that...progression [in mathematics] is maintained by accessing content through a lower linguistic level (Quadrant 3)
gradually working towards higher linguistic demands (Quadrant 4).*

(Coyle, 2007, page 555)

In the case study below you can see how a class of Year 2 children were learning aspects of
measurement within a CLIL approach, including mass and capacity, through a cooking activity.
The trainee teacher, Aimee, had learnt French up until GCSE level.

Case study: Teaching measurement within a CLIL approach

As part of her placement, Aimee had observed her class teacher during a Key Stage
1 after-school French club. She noticed many of the Year 2 children she was
teaching attended and so Aimee decided to brush up on her GCSE French.

→

With encouragement, Aimee planned a mathematics and French lesson where, with the teacher's support, the children baked muffins using as much French vocabulary as she could recall. From her observations she knew many of the children were able to use numbers in French up to 100. She decided to use these numbers and introduce measurement units to the children. Figure 4.2 shows copies of the notes that she carried with her during the lesson. You can see how she has annotated them during discussion with the teacher.

ENGLISH	FRENCH
I like cooking.	J'aime bien faire la cuisine.
flour	farine
sugar	sucre
egg	œuf
baking powder	levure
cocoa powder	cacao en poudre
butter	beurre
teaspoon	cuiller - *object spoon*. cuillerée - *measurement*.
millilitre	millilitre
grams	gramme
degrees	degrés
minute	minute

Numbers 1-100

1	2	3	4	5	6	7	8	9	10
un	deux	trois	quatre	cinq	six	sept	huit	neuf *neuf*	dix
11	12	13	14	15	16	17	18	19	20
onze	douze	treize	quatorze	quinze	seize	dix-sept	dix-huit	dix-neuf *neuf*	vingt
21	22								30
vingt et un	vingt-deux								trente
									40
									quarante
									50
									cinquante
									60
									soixante
									70
									soixante-dix
71								79	80
Soixante et onze								Soixante-dix-neuf *neuf*	quatre-vingts
81								89	90
quatre-vingt-un								quatre-vingt-neuf *neuf*	quatre-vingt-dix
91								99	100
quatre-vingt-onze								quatre-vingt-dix-neuf *neuf*	cent

Figure 4.2

This approach to learning and using mathematics and MFL shows how there has been a very explicit and focused emphasis on mathematical vocabulary in French by the trainee. By going through this process, Aimee developed her own subject knowledge about units of measurement, the number system and also her French vocabulary. This in turn ensured a focus for the children on the mathematical vocabulary being used in this measurement lesson.

Activity

Look at our adaptation of Coyle's CLIL matrix from the earlier research focus (Figure 4.1). Reflect on what lessons in quadrants 1, 2, 3 and 4 might be like.

In which quadrant would you place Aimee's lesson from the case study above? Might the lesson's placement on the graph be different for children who did and did not attend the after-school French club?

Given your own subject knowledge of mathematics and foreign language(s), in which quadrants could you lead lessons?

Now look at the number prompt sheet Aimee made herself (Figure 4.2). What do you notice about how she has structured the table? Why did she not have to write all the numbers out? Why do you think she chose to write out the numbers she did?

Regardless of whether or not your teaching is carried out using a CLIL approach, the key is that you should have the same attention to detail when using and modelling appropriate vocabulary in all lessons. Imagine a lesson where the children are weighing a series of objects. If you ask them what the scale shows, without modelling the units and expecting them to use the units themselves, then you have missed a key learning opportunity. Compare the two variations of the same conversation. Which do you feel is the most effective?

Conversation A	Conversation B
Teacher: What is the mass of this object? Child: It weighs 1.7 Teacher: 1.7 what? Child: 1.7 kilograms Teacher: Good, 1.7 kilograms. If you know that this has a mass of 1.7 kilograms, which of these other objects do you think have a greater weight? Child: I think that object will weigh more. Teacher: How many kilograms more? Child: I think at least half a kilogram heavier.	Teacher: What is the mass of this object? Child: It weighs 1.7 Teacher: 1.7? Child: Yeah, 1.7 Teacher: Good, 1.7. If you know that this weighs 1.7, which of these other objects do you think will weigh more? Child: I think that one will weigh more. Teacher: How many more? Child: I think at least a half more.

We hope that you would agree that even in this very short snippet of the potentially same interaction, Conversation A was a lot richer in terms of the language that was used by both the teacher and the child in relation to kilograms and also other aspects of measurement such as distinguishing between weight and mass. For further discussion, see the section on mass and weight later in this chapter.

Length and area

Length was one of the earliest measures to be used and the cubit (from *cubitum* in Latin) was used to describe this length. Originally a cubit was defined as the length between the elbow and the tip of the index finger, but this was a non-standard measure (because every adult's forearm is a different length) and so the Babylonians created a more accurate cubit measurement. The cubit used in Ancient Egyptian times was made up of 28 parts (seven 'palms' divided into four 'digits') and measured between 52.3cm and 52.4cm long (Dieter, 2003). Although this is no longer used as a measurement, the children you teach may well have heard of it through reading about the building of Noah's Ark or in other historical documents. Children find exploring other measurements that were originally related to our bodies (such as the 'hand', still used to measure the height of horses today) very interesting. Looking at the ratios between different body parts can also develop children's understanding of the proportions of the human body and art (such as drawing portraits of the face or learning about *Vitruvian Man* drawn by Leonardo Da Vinci) or history (such as ancient architecture).

The following case study illustrates how one trainee teacher encouraged children to use and apply measurement of length and area in a design technology unit inspired by their history topic, where the children are using mm, cm and cm^2 which are two units related to one-dimensional (length) and a two-dimensional (area) measurement.

Case Study: Designing Ancient Greek sandals

Halle had visited her Year 5 placement class to help her prepare for her placement where the term's topic was Ancient Greece. On talking about the units she was expected to teach, her class teacher, Alan, advised her to take an integrated approach to mathematics and design and technology.

In preparation for her second planning visit, Halle searched for some pre-existing plans for a DT ancient sandals unit, and came across one that she thought was very good in the TES Connect Resources (**www.tes.co.uk/teaching-resource/D-and-T-Ancient-Sandals-Unit-Years-5-or-6-6019620/**). She liked the planning and resources and she could see how they encouraged the children to think about all the aspects of the design process as well as to use appropriate terminology and thought that this would be a good starting point to plan appropriately for the children in her placement class. However, the resource did not explicitly mention mathematics so she made notes to take on her return to school (see Figure 4.3).

→

Figure 4.3 Halle's design technology and mathematics planning sheet

Halle's second meeting with her class teacher went well. Simon praised Halle's initial ideas. He particularly liked her focus on accurate measurement, and linking length and area. He encouraged Halle to use her ideas in the unit, integrating DT and measurement.

Links to the National Curriculum

The design and technology unit that Halle had downloaded from the internet ensured that through the whole unit the children were developing, planning and communicating a number of ideas related to the Greek sandals. Specifically, the objectives that related to Halle's integrated planning with mathematics included: plan what they have to do, suggesting a sequence of actions and alternatives, if needed (1c); measure, mark out, cut and shape a range of materials, and assemble, join and combine components and materials accurately (2d).

The mathematics objectives that Halle identified were specifically related to measures. In terms of using and applying measures, the children would be able to recognise the need for standard units of measurement (Ma3 1a), approach spatial problems flexibly, including trying alternative approaches to overcome difficulties (Ma3 1c), and use mathematical reasoning to explain features of shape and space (Ma3 1h).

In addition to these skills of use and application, the children were also recognising the need for standard units of length (Ma3 4a), and choosing and using suitable measuring instruments for a task (Ma3 4b).

Halle's planning in the case study above looked at area of irregular shapes – the sole of the sandals. The area of a figure, such as the outline of a child's foot, is measured in the number of squares or, more accurately, in cm^2. Unlike length, which is a measurement in one dimension, area is a measurement in 2D space.

Angle

Another measurement that is carried out in 2D space is angle. An angle is created when two rays share an endpoint. At that point the vertex is created and it is that distance between the two rays at the vertex that can be measured in degrees. At times angles are static, and at others, the angle is dynamic as the research focus below demonstrates.

Research Focus: Learning about angle in Norway

In Norway, the learning of angle concepts in primary school is carried out as an integrated part of the children's physical activity (Fyhn, 2008). In doing so, the children learn that there are two ways of considering an angle: both as a measurement between two static sides and as the process of change in direction.

Fyhn (2008) used a class climbing trip to research how 12-year-olds develop their understanding of angle. She explains that by climbing, *your body forms and reforms angles by making different shapes* (page 19), taking advantage of the fact that *human mathematics is embodied, it is grounded in bodily experience in the world* (Lakoff and Nunez, 2000, cited in Fyhn, page 21). She hoped that the children would be able to identify some of these angles (created by the children's joints, the ropes and the climbing wall, floor and roof) and that these in turn could be used as a resource in a later mathematics lesson, because she knew that *context problems are intended for supporting ... [children] to come to grips with formal mathematics* (page 20).

The children wrote and drew about their climbing trip and Fyhn analysed their work. In doing so, she identified three levels of understanding: recognition of angles, description of angles and using angles as a contextual tool.

$\rightarrow$

> Just as your tutors will expect you to be analytical in your academic work, rather than narrative, Fyhn saw that within the three levels of recognition, description and contextual tool the pupils were either narrative or analytical. Her article explains how she intends to develop the children's analytical understanding further next time she teaches angle through climbing.

Just as the children in Fyhn's class developed their understanding of angle through climbing, history has developed angle through need to use and apply it. The following section looks at time, beginning with how historical use of angle has impacted on how we read analogue clocks.

Time

Up to this point we have considered the dimensions of shape. Now, we consider time, which is thought of as another dimension, and not part of the dimensions we find in shape and space. However, there are several relationships, for example when scientists investigate the notion of space-time, where space and time (as a fourth dimension) are brought together for complex mathematical and physical theories. At a simpler level, we can see how the notion of angle we have just left has had an impact on the way we read and use time.

> ### Activity
> Jot down the links that you can think of between angle and time. Do you know how these links came about?

Why we use analogue time

The Babylonians lived in Mesopotamia, which was an ancient state with societies that lived for around 3000 years between 5000–2100 BC (Pollock, 1999). Their number system was in base 60 (sexagesimal) and this is the reason that we have 60 minutes in an hour, a 24-hour day and 360 degrees in a circle. Let's look at the relationship between circles and time a little more.

The Babylonians counted by 60s (which is 5×12 – how the scale on the face of the analogue clock is constructed). By the Babylonians finding sixtieths we got minutes (*partes minutae* in Latin), and by finding sixtieths of sixtieths (1/3600) we got seconds (*partes minutae secundae* in Latin) (Seligman, online). Although the Babylonians used base 60 for all aspects of their life, it is only within the division of time and degrees that it continues today. The Babylonian numerals were also fraught with complexity in a way that the Hindu-Arabic number system was not and therefore the latter became more popular.

Earlier in this chapter the second was identified as the SI unit for time. Up until 1967 the definition of a second was *the fraction 1/31,556,925.9747 of the tropical year for 1900 January 0 at 12 hours ephemeris time* (Rañada and Tiemblo, 2008, page 459). If you think that was difficult to interpret, then the amended definition of *the duration of 9,192,631,770 periods of*

the radiation corresponding to the transition between the two hyperfine levels of the ground state of
the caesium 133 atom (Rañada and Tiemblo, 2008, page 460) may be beyond you! We hope
that in sharing this with you, it is possible to see 'how time stands still for no man' and how
the pursuit of increasing accuracy continues to be possible due to scientific and mathematical
thinking.

Activity

List as many units of time as you can you identify. We challenge you to come up
with more than 20.

How did you get on? There is a self-assessment question at the end of this chapter that asks the
same question. If you want to have a look at the 25 terms we have identified, see the answers at
the back of this book.

Children need to be aware of all the different aspects of time: hours, minutes, days, years,
decades, etc. They need to understand that using number to describe time means thinking in a
different base than the base 10 they use for counting. It involves the use of fractions when
referring to quarter to and quarter past but equally it involves the use of different language to
mean the same thing. Table 4.1 illustrates a few examples of this.

6:15	Six fifteen	Quarter past six
11:35	Eleven thirty-five	Twenty five to twelve
9:45	Nine forty-five	Quarter to ten

Table 4.1 Language use related to time

Furthermore, two concepts are related to time. The cross-curricular planning that you arrange
should ensure that both are explored. These are reading time (as related to the development of
the analogue clock above) and the passing of time.

Reading time

Rowland (2008, page 155) provides an example of how it is difficult for children to learn to
read time. He shares the following story:

> *Daniel, aged 4, pointed to the clock on the wall and said 'The little hand is on twelve*
> *and the big hand is on ten. What time is it?'. I was reluctant to answer, because this*
> *example also confuses the role of variables – it is a mere accident, a coincidence, that*
> *the minute hand is on the numeral 10 at 'ten to'.*

In addition to the analogue clock, children constantly see digital and 24-hour clocks in their
everyday life, such as on television, microwave, computer or alarm clock displays. You can help
children see the links between displaying time in these different ways by using real-life contexts.
One example is ordering photographs of different times and matching them to events that the

children might do at that time. More authentically, emailing children in another part of the world (for another purpose) or scrutinising an important world event that occurred elsewhere will naturally raise interest in time zone.

The passing of time

They say that 'time flies when you're having fun' and perhaps this is why time is very difficult to estimate. To help children experience the passing of time, it can be effectively embedded within cross-curricular contexts. For example, in physical education children may be timing each other to assess their running speed or in science they may be timing an experiment that is taking place (in seconds, minutes, hours, days or weeks, depending on the experiment). Thinking about the duration of notes and the tempo of a piece of music is related to time. Time can be explored through writing by sequencing events in a piece of creative writing, or thinking about the plot of a book that has been read. Design and technology and art may require waiting for materials to dry. The use of ICT helps us to be more efficient in our tasks. History is an obvious conduit for looking at chronology, but it is also possible to think about time in relation to millennia, centuries, decades, years, months, days, and so on. These different lengths of time mean different things to children of different ages. Geography also enables us to think about the passing of time by looking at the impact that different geographical phenomena have had on the Earth, or the time that it takes to travel to different parts of our local environment or further afield. Issues of sustainability and the impact of pollutants on the planet also offer opportunities for the passing of time to be explored or used.

Volume and capacity, weight and mass

Volume and capacity

Children and trainee teachers often confuse volume and capacity (NCETM, 2010). In Chapter 2 we discussed how some words have an ambiguous meaning, that is they have many meanings in everyday language as well as a more precise mathematical meaning. This is the case with both *volume* and *capacity* as Table 4.2 shows.

Term	Mathematical meaning	Other meanings
Volume	The measure of space (3D) an object occupies	'Turn up the **volume**' in acoustics means the amplitude or loudness 'The **volume** of the hard disk is 50GB' in computing means the storage area 'I read that **volume** last week' in publishing refers to a single text within a collection
Capacity	The measure of liquid that an object is able to hold inside	'I do not have the **capacity** to do any more work' means that there is no more time or resource available to meet the required standard of work. 'The stadium has a **capacity** of 800' means that a maximum of 800 people can attend an event at the stadium 'The **capacity** of my battery is lower when my laptop screen is brighter' means the discharge time

Table 4.2 Definitions of volume and capacity

As you can see, there is some relationship between the two mathematical terms, but this depends on the thickness of the faces. However, as a rule of thumb the volume of an object that is 10cm $\times$ 10cm $\times$ 10cm would be written as $(10cm)^3$, which equates to filling the cube with 1000 cubic centimetres, and its capacity would be 1 litre. Cubic centimetres are used in car engines, for example a car engine of 1400cc is also referred to as a 1.4 litre engine.

Weight and mass

Just as people are confused about volume and capacity, there is also similar confusion between weight and mass.

Mass is the amount of 'stuff' that an object is made up of. The object's *weight*, however, may vary, depending on the force of gravity pulling on it at the time. No matter where we are on Earth the force of gravity is always the same, and that is why it is easy to be confused between the two terms. However, in a location where the gravity is different (say, on the Moon where the gravitational force is weaker) the object would weigh less than it would on Earth.

To illustrate this, imagine a child who has a mass of 35kg. When we weigh the child on Earth, he or she will have a weight of 35kg. However, if the child travelled far out to space where there was no gravitational force, the scales would show the child to weigh 0kg. Their mass would not have changed and they would still have a mass of 35kg.

It is important to make this distinction, albeit a seemingly picky one, because we should not be teaching errors to children.

The case study below illustrates how a meaningful context, sparked by an educational visit, can assist children in considering how weight, mass, volume and capacity are used and applied.

Case Study: The household recycling centre

Mitchell was on placement with a Year 5 class who were studying recycling for the half term. Early in Mitchell's placement, the class were visiting a household recycling centre and Mitchell was keen to draw as many learning experiences as possible from the visit. Although he was not responsible for organising the trip because it had been arranged before he started placement, he was able to accompany the teachers on the recce prior to the school visit.

Having volunteered to plan a unit of mathematics that would begin after the visit, Mitchell was hoping for inspiration from the recce. He was taken with the movement of the waste from households to the centre and how the recycling company dealt with the amount of waste that was brought in during their short visit. He questioned their host, Dan, who explained that each articulated trailer could hold 100 cubic metres, but that to go on the road legally each trailer can only hold around 21 tonnes. Because plastic bottles are light (low in density), a trailer can be fully loaded to capacity. This is the case for cans also. However, paper and

$\rightarrow$

glass are heavier (more dense) and so a trailer would reach its maximum payload of 21 tonnes before being fully loaded (see list below).

Type	Weight per cubic metre
Cans (crushed)	187kg (0.187 tonnes)
Cans (loose)	75kg (0.075 tonnes)
Glass	380kg (0.38 tonnes)
Paper	243kg (0.243 tonne)
Plastic bottles	25kg (0.025 tonnes)

Dan explained that councils collect household recycling waste in a lot of different ways. This means that co-mingled (mixed) waste also gets delivered to the centre. Mitchell asked what the weight of the co-mingled waste per cubic metre would be, and Dan explained that because of the different ratios of materials a lot of the council waste varies in weight. District councils carry out waste analyses on the co-mingle collection rounds to identify the take-up from the residents and the optimal collection methods.

Mitchell could see a number of mathematical opportunities through this discussion with Dan. Following the class visit, under Mitchell's direction the children collected paper, plastic bottles and cans which they placed into designated boxes. When they were full, the children weighed them, alongside a box of glass bottles Mitchell had also brought in.

They worked out how much of each recyclable they could fit into a cubic metre, which they then used to calculate the weight of each.

Mitchell then set the children a problem about co-mingled waste. Using the information they now knew about the weight of the recyclables, he asked them to calculate the weight of a co-mingled load if it contained 25 per cent of each product.

Mitchell and the children continued to look at problems that related to the weight and volume of the materials. For example, if a council collected plastic separately, what would the weight of 33 per cent cans, 33 per cent glass and 33 per cent paper be? Would the maximum payload of the trailer be reached? Using other ratios, how could you fill the trailer up? Not fill it up?

The children's work was fed back to Dan, who wrote to the children thanking them for their interest in sustainability.

Although we only see a snapshot of Mitchell's planning, his way of working unwittingly addressed the interconnected nature of learning about the future of sustainability (see Paige *et al.*, 2008). Paige *et al.* (2008) identify an issue that they claim has inhibited further work in education on this area. They explain how, up until now, each of the disciplines that is concerned with sustainability seems to have worked in isolation. To support this argument they cite literature related to science education, mathematics education, futures education including educating for sustainability, place-based education, trans-disciplinary approaches and the importance of belonging and developing ecological relationships (page 19). Furthermore, the work that Mitchell carried out reflected the distinctive characteristics to ecological place-based learning. These are that it:

- emerges from the particular context of the place;
- is inherently multi-disciplinary;
- is inherently experiential;
- demonstrates an underpinning philosophy of education that is broader than 'learning to earn';
- connects with self and community (Woodhouse and Knapp, 2000).

Using transferable skills

Using cross-curricular opportunities to use and apply or teach mathematics presents opportunities and challenges. One of the opportunities, raised several times in this book already, is the use of transferable skills across different curriculum subjects. This makes good sense because not only are the skills being taught in a meaningful and motivational way, they are also challenging the children in a more natural context. One challenge that arises by planning in this way, however, is that the skills that are used are not necessarily presented to the children in a systematic way because they are introduced on a 'need to know' basis. This is addressed in further detail in Chapter 6.

Although the research literature tells us that it is very complex for humans to transfer knowledge from one context to another, skills can be transferred between National Curriculum content (i.e. be cross-curricular). A number of schools in the UK are beginning to use this approach. For example, the South Norwood Primary School website explains how they believe that they use *an exciting skills-based curriculum that links subjects purposefully and progressively together through exciting and stimulating themes that have a positive appeal to children* (**www.southnorwoodprimaryschool.co.uk/curriculum.htm**).

Reading scales

In this section we look at one of these skills – reading scales. Many view the learning and teaching of measurement in primary school as *the development of a web of related components rather than a unitary construct* where children's learning is *situated within forms of teaching practices and meditational means* (Koehler, 2002, page 156). Typically, the order of measurement taught in primary schools follows an order related to dimension, for example one dimension (length), two dimensions (area), three dimensions (volume). The case study below explores how children are using a transferable skill – reading scales – to learn about some scientific notions that do not fit neatly into the more traditional way of teaching mathematics, but have a more profound effect on the children's learning of these complex ideas (Hickman and Kiss, 2010).

Case Study: Weather station

Veronica was on placement just after Easter in a Year 3 class. When she had arrived there was great excitement among the children because before the school holiday they had written to the local BBC radio station about their weather station. The BBC had responded by contacting the head teacher about visiting the school to broadcast a feature on the school. The BBC wanted the class to be able to describe on air how they had designed the weather station and what they were learning from using it.

Veronica's help was enlisted immediately and with a group of children she asked them to identify the features of the weather station. She was genuinely surprised at the amount that the children had learnt over the previous two terms. She was also concerned that the children's vocabulary and scientific knowledge was greater than hers, and worried that they had to spell some of the technical terms for her. Figure 1.4 is a photograph of the flip chart sheet that Veronica populated during her discussion with a mixed-attainment group of children.

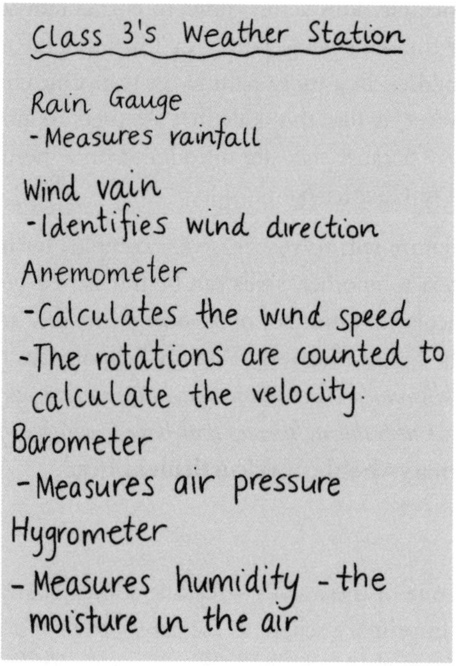

Class 3's Weather Station

Rain Gauge
- Measures rainfall

Wind vain
- Identifies wind direction

Anemometer
- Calculates the wind speed
- The rotations are counted to calculate the velocity.

Barometer
- Measures air pressure

Hygrometer
- Measures humidity - the moisture in the air

Figure 4.4 Class 3's discussion record about their weather station

→

After school, Veronica spoke with her class teacher, Tony, who was a mathematics specialist teacher (MaST – see Chapter 8 for more about MaST teachers). Veronica suggested that the focus of the BBC's visit should be on science. However, Tony was keen to showcase how mathematics was used in the construction and applied while the children collected data from the weather station, as well as ICT, where the data were uploaded frequently on to the school's website. The children and Tony were very proud that they identified trends and made predictions for a weather forecast, which was sometimes more accurate than the BBC's!

Links to the National Curriculum

Weather is a topic that lends itself to addressing a multitude of National Curriculum objectives. For example, in this case study alone, we could see how in geography children in Key Stage 2 are expected to collect and record evidence (1b), to communicate in ways that are appropriate to the audience and use appropriate vocabulary (1e, 2a), to use appropriate field work techniques (2c) and explain why places are like they are, for example in terms of weather (3d).

In science, Key Stage 2 children are expected to undertake scientific enquiry that includes asking questions that can be investigated scientifically and decide how to find answers (2a), consider what sources of information they will use to answer questions (2b), and check observations and measurements by repeating them where appropriate (2h). Furthermore, children are expected to make comparisons and identify simply patterns or associations (2i), use observations and measurements or other data (2j), decide whether these conclusions agree with any prediction made and/or they enable further predictions to be made (2l).

In relation to ICT, the children were using simulations and exploring models to find their weather predictions (2c), they were sharing and exchanging information on the blog, thinking carefully about the audience (3a, 3b) and were working with a range of information to consider its purpose (5a) and working with others (5b).

Finally, for mathematics, there were significant elements of using and applying, including making connections (Ma2 1a), recognising the need for standard units of measurement (Ma3 1a), and presenting and interpreting solutions to problems (Ma3 1h). Furthermore, the children were understanding measure (Ma3 4a, 4b) and handling data (Ma4 1a, 1c, 1h; Ma4 2a, 2b).

Not only does the case study above show how certain skills can be used transferably in different contexts, it also demonstrates the children's understanding of several mathematical concepts addressed in one cross-curricular activity.

Learning Outcomes Review

This chapter has encouraged you to consider a number of aspects of measurement. The concepts that children must understand in order to use and apply measures are estimation, conservation and transitive reasoning. Without these, measurement is not going to be able to be used and applied with meaning. The chapter has also explored the need for using appropriate language, transferable skills and standardised measures. Content areas of the National Curriculum such as length and area, angle, time, volume and capacity, as well as weight and mass have been discussed.

Self-assessment questions

1. How many units of time can you identify?
2. If you speak another language, think about how the number system is expressed in that language. What are the similarities and differences to English? If you do not speak another language then use the internet to help you to do this.
3. What does the term *conservation* mean?

Further Reading

Johnstone, R. and McKinstry, R. (2008) *Immersion in a second language at school.* This is the final report of the evaluation of the Early Partial Immersion in French at Walker Road Primary School, Aberdeen. It is available at **www.strath.ac.uk/media/faculties/hass/scilt/publications/SCILT_2001_Johnstone_Immersion.pdf**

References

Andreou, Y. and Kotsis, K.T. (2005) The estimation of length, surface area, and volume by blind and sighted children. *Vision 2005 – Proceedings of the International Congress held 4–7 April 2005 in London, UK.* Volume 1282: 780–784.

Babai, R. (2009) Piagetian on cognitive level and the tendency to use intuitive rules when solving comparison tasks. *International Journal of Science and Mathematics Education*, 8 (2): 203–221.

CNN (1999) *Metric mishap caused loss of NASA orbiter.* Available at **http://articles.cnn.com/1999-09-30/tech/9909_30_mars.metric.02_1_climate-orbiter-spacecraft-team-metric-system?_s=PM:TECH** (accessed 13/3/11).

Coyle, D. (2007) Content and language integrated learning: towards a connected research agenda for CLIL pedagogies. *The Integrated Journal or Bilingual Education and Bilingualism*, 10, (5): 543–562.

Dieter, A. (2003). *The Encyclopaedia of Ancient Egyptian Architecture*. Princeton, NJ: Princeton University Press.

Fourier, J. (1822) *Théorie analytique de la chaleur*. Paris: Firmin Didot.

Frantsuz, E.T. (2010) Fundamental physical constants in the new international system of units (SI). *Measurement techniques,* 53 (3): 228–231.

Fyhn, A. (2008) A climbing class' reinvention of angles. *Educational Studies in Mathematics,* 67 (1): 19–35.

Grin (2005) cited in Coyle, D. (2007) Content and language integrated learning: towards a connected research agenda for CLIL pedagogies. *The Integrated Journal of Bilingual Education and Bilingualism,* 10 (5): 543–562.

Hickman, R. and Kiss, L. (2010) Cross-curricular gallery learning: A phenomenological case study. *International Journal of Art and Design Education,* 29 (1): 27–36.

Koehler, M.J. (2002) Designing case-based hypermedia for developing understanding of children's mathematical reasoning. *Cognition and Instruction,* 20(2): 151–195.

Long, K. and Kamii, C. (2001) The measurement of time: children's construction of transitivity, unit iteration and conservation of speed. *School Science and Mathematics,* 101 (3): 125–132.

NCETM (2010) Measure – Volume and capacity. *Primary Magazine* Issue 20. Available at **https://www.ncetm.org.uk/resources/22757** (accessed 16/3/11).

New Scientist (2009) NASA attacked for sticking to imperial units. *New Scientist,* 202 (2713).

Paige, K., Lloyd, D. and Chartres, M. (2008) Moving towards transdisciplinarity: An ecological sustainable focus for science and mathematics pre-service education in the primary/middle years. *Asia-Pacific Journal of Teacher Education,* 36 (1): 19–33.

Piaget, J. and Inhelder, B. (1974) *The child's construction of quantities: Conservatism and atomism*. London: Routledge.

Pollock, S. (1999) *Ancient Mesopotamia*. Cambridge: Cambridge University Press.

QCDA (2009) *Mathematics Test A KS2 Levels 3-5*. Available at **https://orderline.qcda.gov.uk/gempdf/9999098169/1849621020.pdf** (accessed 17/3/11).

Ramos-Christian, V., Schleser, R. and Varn, M.E. (2008) Math fluency: accuracy versus speed in preoperational and concrete operational first and second grade children. *Early Childhood Education Journal,* 35: 543–549.

Rañada, A.F. and Tiemblo, A. (2008) Time, clocks and parametric invariance. *Foundations of Physics,* 38: 458–469.

Rowland, T. (2008) The purpose, use and design of examples. *Educational Studies in Mathematics,* 69: 149–163.

Seligman, C. (online) Timekeeping. Available at **http://cseligman.com/text/sky/time.htm** (accessed 13/3/11).

Siegler, R.S. and Booth, J.L. (2004) Development of numerical estimation in young children. *Child Development*, 75 (2): 428–444.

Woodhouse, J. and Knapp, C. (2000) *Place-based curriculum and instruction: Outdoor and environmental education approaches*. Charleston, WV: ERIC Clearinghouse on Rural Education and Small Schools (ERIC Document Reproduction Service No. ED448012) .

Wright, B.C., Robertson, S. and Hadfield, L. (2011) Transitivity for height versus speed: To what extent do the under-7s really have a transitive capacity? *Thinking and Reasoning*, 17 (1): 57–81.

5. Handling data

Learning Outcomes

This chapter explores:
- how the need to handle data developed;
- embedding the data-handling cycle;
- posing questions;
- data collection and analysis;
- primary and secondary data;
- presenting and reflecting on findings.

Professional Standards for QTS

Q14 Have a secure knowledge and understanding of their subjects/curriculum areas and related pedagogy to enable them to teach effectively across the age and ability range for which they are trained.

Q15 Know and understand the relevant statutory and non-statutory curricula and frameworks, including those provided through the National Strategies, for their subjects/curriculum areas, and other relevant initiatives applicable to the age and ability range for which they are trained.

Q17 Know how to use skills in literacy, numeracy and ICT to support their teaching and wider professional activities.

Q23 Design opportunities for learners to develop their literacy, numeracy and ICT skills.

Q25 (b) Build on prior knowledge, develop concepts and processes, enable learners to apply new knowledge, understanding and skills and meet learning objectives.

Q28 Support and guide learners to reflect on their learning, identify the progress they have made and identify their emerging learning needs.

Introduction

The previous chapters have discussed how reasoning, problem-solving and communication are essential skills needed for children to be able to reflect upon and discuss their work and its quality, and develop their understanding about what they can do to improve it. This chapter will concentrate on how these skills are used in the learning of handling data from a mathematical perspective and how data handling can aid the learning of other subject areas.

Beyond the wider school curriculum, it is also important for you to be aware that other legislation bears down on your professional role. One such policy document is the United

Nations Convention on the Rights of the Child (UNCRC, 1989). In Article 12, point 1 states *the child who is capable of forming his or her own views [has] the right to express those freely in all matters affecting [them], the views of the child being given due weight in accordance with the age and maturity of the child.* This is followed up in Article 13 where *the child shall have the right to freedom of expression; this right shall include freedom to seek, receive and impart information and ideas of all kinds, regardless of frontiers, either orally, in writing or in print, in the form of art, or through any other media of the child's choice.*

Keep these articles from the UNCRC in your mind as you read this chapter. At the end you will be asked how you think the knowledge, skills and understanding that are developed through handling data empower children to enact this right.

How the need to handle data developed

It is only over the past 50 years that handling data (or statistics as it is known in the secondary curriculum) has developed from becoming *almost nothing to becoming both a major part of the mathematics taught to all 5–16 year old children and also an integral part of other school subjects* (Holmes, 2003, page 439). This section explores a little historical background as to why this might be and sets the scene for the remainder of the chapter to demonstrate why using and applying data is such an important skill for primary school children to achieve.

> ### Activity
> Over one day, jot down:
> (a) All the times you access data that has been stored;
> (b) All the times you create data.
> Reflect on the nature of the types of data and your purpose for using them.

When accessing data, you may have listened to the radio, used your mobile phone, watched on-demand television, read journals, magazines or books, searched the internet or accessed a virtual learning environment. When creating data, you may have written texts or emails, tweeted, blogged, shared files, written a shopping list or left a voicemail. Some of the data you created will be temporary, but others may be more permanent.

Historically, humankind also used, and later stored, data for reasons that were similar to the purposes you will have identified.

Statistical projections which speak to the senses without fatiguing the mind, possess the advantage of fixing attention on a great number of important facts (von Humbolt, 1811, cited by Funkhouser, 1937, page 269).

Tally marks

For example, one of the earlier ways of creating and storing data was through the use of tally marks. You will have read in Chapter 2 about the evolution of counting during the Stone Age. Tally marks were used by Stone Age people as a way of recording quantity as early as 30,000 BC. This was proven when, in 1937, the shinbone of a wolf was found that clearly demonstrated the engraving of 55 notches of equal length, arranged in groups of five (Allen, 1997). Although it is not known what was being quantified, what is clear is that quantification was a key component of human existence at that time.

Census data

Census data have been collected in Britain regularly for 200 years, from 1801 to the present day. The first census asked five questions and involved two million households. In 2001 the census covered 24 million households and asked 40 questions. This generated two billion data items (Office for National Statistics, 2001).

The British census evolved out of a perceived need to be able to track issues and use the data as a means to solve potential problems. For example, the first census was taken because there was a growing concern that the growing population might outstrip the country's food supply. In 1891 a question regarding the number of rooms in each house was introduced out of concern for overcrowding in urban areas. The year 1921 saw the introduction of a question regarding 'place of work' as people started to use public transport between suburbs more. The 2001 census introduced a question about religion as it was deemed that people identify themselves as a member of a religious group. This latter question was met with a mixed response. It became knowledge among many of the British population that there was a growing movement requesting people to respond to the religion question by answering 'Jedi'. If you think that this is a ludicrous suggestion, then you will be even more surprised by the response. In fact, 390,000 people responded that their religion was Jedi. This equates to 7 out of every 1,000 people in Britain.

Maps

Maps are another source of data. They are a 2D representation of a 3D environment. They have many mathematical features including the following.

A key
A key is a representation of a feature on the map. Contour lines are used on a map to show the gradient of the land (that is, how steep it is).

Scale
Maps often, but not exclusively (take, for example the London Underground map) use a scale factor that enables the reader of the map to identify the distance represented on a map.

Direction

Most maps that children will experience in primary school, and that you will use in everyday life, use a north/south, east/west convention. This wasn't always the case. For example, in the Middle Ages maps utilised a 'T' and 'O' which represented 'Top' and 'Orient' (derived from Latin, *oriens*, meaning east). This meant the top pointed to the west.

Co-ordinates

Cartesian co-ordinates were most notably developed in the seventeenth century by René Descartes. (Note the relationship to his name; Descartes used the name *Cartesius* in Latin.) This was a revelation at the time because it became possible to describe geometric shapes according to their position in 2D and then 3D space. Cartesian co-ordinates were the foundation for many branches of mathematics that are used today such as linear algebra, differential geometry and group theory as well as other disciplines such as astronomy, engineering and computer design. Enabling children to have a sound foundation in co-ordinates enables them to develop thinking in these areas later on.

Longitude and latitude

Latitude was relatively straightforward for mathematicians to calculate because the equator was the most obvious starting position. On the other hand, longitude was far more difficult to identify, particularly at sea. First, there was no obvious starting point and so for many centuries explorers used their own capital city as the reference point. This was rectified as late as 1884 when it was universally agreed to use the Greenwich meridian as the zero point of longitude. Furthermore, identifying the longitude at sea was very complicated indeed. Even though Galileo Galilei suggested in 1612 that the orbit of the moons of Jupiter could be used accurately enough to find longitude, practically this was difficult to achieve. John Harrison invented the marine chronometer in 1773 but because it was so expensive to produce, cartographers continued to use the Moon as they had done for centuries. Although marine chronometers eventually became cheaper to use, it was really only in the late 1880s when radio waves became widespread that measurement of longitude became much easier for ocean-goers.

More recently, satellite navigation systems make navigation very simple indeed, from using a mobile phone application to walk to a particular location, to printing out a route planner to guide a driver to a further location.

Maps contain a lot of data and using a map effectively means using a lot of mathematical knowledge, skills and understanding. For example, when making a choice about which route to take, you need to be able to:

● interpret the symbols;

● use the scale factor to calculate the distance;

● know which direction to travel in (do you hold a map in the direction you are travelling so you know to turn left or right, or do you keep it 'upright' at all times?).

You may also need to take into consideration:

- the impact of the recent heavy rain on the normally small stream running alongside your preferred walking route;
- the fitness of your walking companions and the terrain;
- time of day – heavy traffic.

Data storage

Relatively recently, data containing more information have been stored. For example, in 1725, Basile Bouchon used a perforated paper loop in a drawloom to store patterns that were to be woven into fabric in a repeated fashion. About 150 years later, punch cards and punch tapes were commonly used. In the middle of the last century, magnetic tape was used to store data and by the 1970s the compact cassette and the floppy disc were developed. Around the same time the laser disc was available on the market but this was soon superseded by the compact disc (CD) and the digital versatile disc (DVD). Very recently, blue-violet laser has brought about the Blu-ray disc. In the future, the holographic versatile disc (HVD) may be the next generation of data storage, being able to hold 160 times more data than a Blu-ray disc (**http://gadgets.fosfor.se/history-of-data-storage/**).

The information age

The discussion above demonstrates how, particularly in the last 30 years, the increase in the amount of information available and the increasingly easier way that information flows have led to what is commonly referred to as the information age. With this easy access to information, it is even more crucial that people are able to handle data to ensure they are able to critically evaluate data by knowing the intended audience, purpose and origins in order to evaluate the validity and reliability of the data. For a further discussion on this, read Chapter 8.

Developments in information have even led to a relatively new branch of applied mathematics, information theory, which began by looking at the quantification of information. It has a direct involvement in your own life as a student because it is used in data compression (e.g. zip and pdf files) and plagiarism software. It also has applications further afield such as helping to understand black holes! (Collins, 2002).

Implications for teaching and learning

The above brief outline of only a few aspects of the development of data and data storage illustrates the need for children to be well equipped to confidently, efficiently and effectively evaluate and process data. The remaining sections of this chapter look at how you can develop children's understanding in handling data across the curriculum.

Data handling across the curriculum

It is likely that you will have come across the data-handling cycle elsewhere in your course or your own schooling. Very simply put, it is a cyclical process that contains three elements which could be equated simply to 'plan', 'do', 'review'. See Figure 5.1.

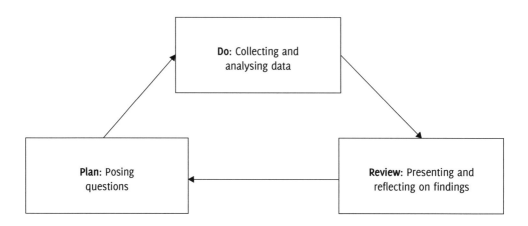

Figure 5.1 The data handling cycle

We suggest that it is possible to observe this simple three-stage data-handling cycle in many of the other aspects of your role as a trainee teacher and teacher. Notice how the planning cycle (Figure 5.2) and the science investigation process (Figure 5.3) both reflect the 'plan', 'do', 'review' elements.

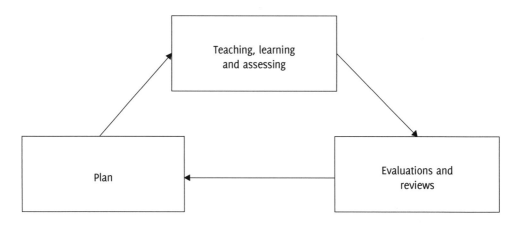

Figure 5.2 The planning cycle

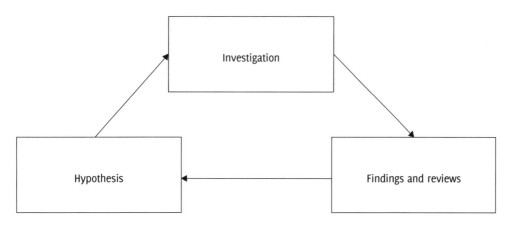

Figure 5.3 The science investigation cycle

Crucially for all the cycles, one element (review) is an evaluation/revision of the process carried out. If necessary, the cycle will continue, until the desired outcome is achieved. For the data handling cycle the evaluation question is 'Have we answered the question we set out to answer?' In the planning cycle, one evaluation question might be 'Have the children achieved the desired learning outcome?' The science investigation cycle asks, 'Have we been able to prove/disprove our hypothesis?' In all cases, if the answer is 'no' or 'we need to find out more' then amendments are made and further data collection, planning or investigations are undertaken.

Links to the National Curriculum

The review element particularly requires problem solving and reasoning skills to be utilised. The programme of study for handling data requires Key Stage 2 children to be able to *approach problems flexibly, including trying alternative approaches to overcome any difficulties* (Ma4 1b) and *explain and justify their methods and reasoning* (Ma4 1h) (DfES, 1999, page 73).

We have presented Figures 5.1, 5.2 and 5.3 as oversimplified 'plan', 'do', 'review' three-stage processes. While we certainly acknowledge that they are each far more complex and detailed, we hope you begin to see similar three-stage processes in many of the tasks you undertake as a trainee teacher. The data-handling process seems to pervade many subjects of the curriculum and your professional life. This chapter looks specifically at the National Curriculum, taking different aspects of the data-handling cycle to discuss in more detail. Another example might be the research process you carry out where you identify a research question, carry out small-case research to explore the issues, reflect on the findings in relation to your question and your wider pedagogy. Chapters 7 and 8 look at how data are utilised in your wider professional role.

Although we start this part of the chapter with 'posing questions' it is important to note that when you are teaching handling data to children, or when they are using handling data skills to learn about other subjects, the children may not necessarily have to follow the process through in its entirety every time.

Posing questions

Activity

We ask questions and then informally or formally draw on data to answer those questions. The table here provides some questions. Think about how you might answer them using both informal and formal data. The first one offers some suggestions to how you may respond.

Question	Informal	Formal
How old is my father's older brother?	I know Dad is 56 and his brother is about 2 years older than him. Dad's birthday is next month, but his brother's is two months later. So, my uncle is 58 but he'll be 59 in about three months' time.	Ask Dad what his brother's date of birth is. Look up the family's birth certificates. Phone uncle to ask his date of birth. Refer to Mum's birthday book where it will be listed.
Shall I hang out the washing today?		
What time shall I leave home to take the train from Leeds to Manchester?		
When do I have to buy my next car tax disc?		
How much is a litre of milk?		
What will happen if I stop my medication?		

The questions above have varying levels of stake involved in answering them. For example, having an out-of-date tax disc is probably more significant than remembering an uncle's age. Stopping medication without medical guidance could have the most significant outcome.

The activity above was designed to develop your awareness of the number of questions you ask every day as well as the range of ways in which you may decide to answer them. Research shows us how young children, because of their enquiring nature, tend to ask even more questions than adults (Frazier *et al.*, 2009). However, other research shows us that sadly, very quickly during primary school, children start to ask fewer and fewer questions (see Research Focus below).

Research Focus

Molinero and García-Madruga (2011, page 26) state *the ability and the motivation for question asking are, or should be, some of the most important aims of*

$\rightarrow$

education. However, their research has identified that this is not necessarily the case for secondary students: *unfortunately students neither ask many questions, nor good ones*. They cite the following reasons for this.

- Teachers have the monopoly on questions.
- Children may think that asking a question demonstrates to their peers they are not as capable.

Furthermore, their research found that:

- children ask a question in school on average once a day;
- these are usually shallow questions (for example, 'what does that word mean?');
- test-driven curricula reduce the number of questions children ask.

Although the research is related to older children, it resonates with our experience of visiting hundreds of ITT trainees operating in primary classrooms and also with the expectations we observe of trainee teachers early in their course.

Interestingly, Molinero and García-Madruga's research revealed that children ask more questions the more they know about a topic. This is called the 'gap factor' where gaps in knowledge become more obvious and the child wants to fill them. They also identified that attitude towards information is a key component in asking questions. We return to these two revelations later in the chapter.

Chapter 2 also highlighted the positive impact that encouraging children to ask questions has on their motivation to learn, as well as offering you a rich opportunity for assessing their knowledge and understanding. So, when you are working with children, by listening to their questions you are in the privileged position to be able to identify what their interests are and to build on them to plan motivational, interesting lessons across a given time. The case study below demonstrates how Shelley was fascinated by the questions her Year 1 children asked when given the opportunity.

Case Study: Winter

Shelley was on placement with a class of Year 1 children for eight weeks. During that time they were using 'Winter' as a theme and she had identified that the children were particularly interested in the effect that winter had on (a) the environment and (b) on themselves. These two areas of interest led Shelley to use data-handling skills, knowledge and understanding with the children when they posed the following questions.

- What birds visited the birdfeed fat balls we made and took home?
- What type of materials are our winter clothes made of? Why?

$\rightarrow$

- Some trees are deciduous and others are evergreen. Do you see more of one type or the other on your way to school?

- How many worms do we find in the garden in winter? What about in summer? Why do we think there is such a difference?

- After looking at photos of how the children were dressed when they went outside over the Christmas vacation: What would happen if we did not wear warm clothes in winter?

- When do we not wear warm clothes in winter? Why does that not have the same effect? (For example, swimming costume in the local council indoor baths, wearing a t-shirt in the house when the heating is on.)

During that time, Shelley spoke with her mentor about how the children posing the questions themselves, with Shelley's support, motivated them to be fully involved in the learning activities. The questions were sometimes more complex than she had thought Year 1 children could capably respond to, and they enabled her to address objectives from the medium-term plan from a range of other subjects (see Links to the National Curriculum below) highly effectively, while also meeting objectives from the mathematics programme of study.

Links to the National Curriculum

The above case study is an example of how listening to and planning around children's responses can enable you to teach in a way that is relevant and meaningful to the children.

Shelley was able to cover many areas of the curriculum including the following.

Mathematics: Processing, representing and interpreting data (Ma2);
Count reliably up to 20, extending to 100 and beyond (2a);
Solve a relevant problem by using simple lists, tables and charts to sort, classify and organise information (5a).

Science: Life processes and living things (Sc2);
Humans and other animals need food and water to stay alive (2b);
Find out about the different kinds of plants and animals in the local environment (5a).

Geography: Knowledge and understanding of pattern and process;
Recognise changes in physical and human features (4b).

To summarise, ensure that the questions posed during handling data opportunities are contexts that are 'real' (authentic) and therefore more likely to be motivational to the children. Where possible, develop questions with the children that link to the theme being studied at the time.

There are two words of warning in relation to this recommendation. The first is that questions linked to a current theme should be used to provide answers to real problems or questions, not be a superficial link for the sake of it. More frequently seen is the second. Asking children to identify their own questions can provide superficial questions that do not support them to learn more advanced data collection, analysis and presentation. For example, we have seen Year 6 children collecting the colour of passing cars using tally marks, when we know they had also undertaken those methods many years earlier.

Data collection and analysis

In many primary mathematics books data collection and data analysis are treated as discrete sections. While it is true that you must have data before they can be analysed, we present them here together. This is because it is essential that you guide children to collect data appropriately so that they can effectively analyse them in order to answer their question. Data collection, however it is carried out, can be a very time-consuming and intensive process. How devastating it is for children and trainee teachers alike when all their hard work then does not reveal the intended outcome!

Data collection

> ### Activity
> The table below offers some methods of data collection. You may have used some of these yourself at school or during your own practitioner research. If possible, work with a small group of trainees to consider the strengths and limitations of using each method with primary aged children. Remember to think about what the children themselves would gain from using each strategy, as well as the practicalities that some of the methods will throw up.
>
> | Method of data collection | Strengths | Limitations |
> | --- | --- | --- |
> | Observation | | |
> | Experiment | | |
> | Obtaining data from a valid and reliable published source | | |
> | Obtaining data from any internet site | | |
> | Paper-based questionnaires | | |
> | Interviews | | |
> | Internet questionnaires (e.g. www.surveymonkey.com) | | |

If you would like to read further about the methods listed in the table above, refer to the Further Reading section at the end of this chapter for recommendations.

Using primary data sources

The case study below shows an example of how children collected their own data. It may also help you to think further about some of the methods of data collection used in this particular situation.

Activity

As you are reading the case study below, think about how you would work with the Year 5 children to resolve their concerns. Why do you think Samir encouraged them to use mean and mode as a way of analysing their data?

Case Study: The healthy snack bar

One Thursday, some of the children in the Year 5 class complained to Samir, their trainee teacher, about the queue at the school's snack bar at playtime. They explained that by the time they had bought their snack and eaten it, they had no time to go out and play.

Samir asked them if they would like to undertake some data collection to provide evidence to take to the Year 6 class who ran the bar. When they agreed, Samir promised she would talk with them further the next day.

Samir discussed the incident with her mentor and together they agreed that Samir could amend the planned mathematics lesson slightly so that an extended plenary would involve a class discussion of the issue and what data would need to be collected.

During the lesson plenary, a table was collaboratively produced and agreement was reached about a rota for collecting the data.

Day: Mon/Tues/Wed/Thurs/Fri	Number of servers: 1/2/3/4/__
Time:	Number of children in queue:
10:15	
10:17	
10:19	
10:21	
10:23	
10:25	
Mode of children in the queue today: _____	Mean of children in the queue today: _____

→

A week later, the data had been collected and the children compared these with the number of children serving.

Day	Number of servers	Mode	Mean
Monday	3	14	11
Tuesday	2	17	16
Wednesday	2	20	17
Thursday	3	13	12
Friday	3	16	15

The children noticed that on the two days where only two children were serving, the mean number of children waiting was higher, as was the modal number of children waiting. They also identified that although the mode was also quite high when there were three servers, the mean number of children waiting was lower. They discussed why this might be the case and agreed that although there were a large number of children waiting at times, the serving time was reduced because of the third server. They agreed to share their findings with Year 6 and they were invited into their class the following week.

After the findings were presented to them, the Year 6 class explained how two children had gone to play in the week that they should have been serving. Those children stated that they now saw the implications of their actions and the whole class agreed a renewed effort when it was their turn to serve in the snack bar. The class also noticed that Friday appeared a busier day and they were going to return to their class to look at the data they had on their selling to see if this was similar to sales on other Fridays. They wondered if they should have additional servers on Fridays.

After the events described in the case study above, Michelle, the head teacher, learned of the work that the children were doing to improve the snack bar waiting times. As a result of this, Michelle awarded the two classes a special recognition certificate during assembly because she wanted to reward the good work that the children had done in using mathematics to improve the children's waiting time. Michelle also asked for two volunteers from each class to present their work to the PTFA committee meeting one evening, because the PTFA had originally set up the snack bar. The PTFA were also impressed with the children's work. Having discussed the findings, they agreed to award serving merits to children who worked in a committed way at the snack bar.

Links to the National Curriculum

The recognition given to the children from the head teacher and the PTFA demonstrates the importance placed on healthy eating (**http://home.healthyschools. gov.uk/**) and on the importance of child voice in a school (National College, 2011). Furthermore, the head teacher was very keen to use the children's work as a way of demonstrating how using and applying mathematics across the school's day develops improved outcomes for all the children who use the healthy snack bar.

PSHE is an area that underpins much of the school curriculum and addresses the issue of healthy eating and offers children the opportunity to make informed choices (3a).

Many areas of mathematics are included in the above case study. One of the most important things for children to gain from this activity was the ability to draw inferences from data in practical activities and recognise the difference between meaningful and misleading representations of data (breadth of study 1e).

Before the case study, you were asked to think about how you might have addressed the children's concerns if you had been on placement in that school. Perhaps you would have simply dismissed their concerns, believing that as a trainee teacher you were powerless to do anything about them. This case study certainly demonstrates that in this case, that was not true. However, whatever course of action you might have taken, think about how data play a part in your own decision-making.

In the case study, primary data were the only type of data that could be used because the problem being solved was so context specific. However, at other times using secondary data may be more appropriate for your intended learning outcomes. At the beginning of this chapter we reminded you that the whole data-handling process does not need to be followed through every time.

Using secondary data sources

Children do not always have to spend time collecting data themselves. As we have already stated, this is a very time-consuming process and could be an unproductive use of their time if quality data are held elsewhere already. Some data will not be able to be easily or safely collected as a primary source by children. This should not mean that they cannot explore the area they wish, but that secondary data could be obtained if possible.

The internet is a very rich source of data for children to use fairly efficiently. You could also provide data for the children that you have collected from the internet yourself if the collection of the data is not part of your learning intentions or if you deem the use of the internet for the data you are collecting to be unsafe for the children. In the case study below we meet Aly, a trainee teacher who used a wide range of data sources with a Year 5 class.

Case Study: Using archive materials

Aly tells us about her 'Victorian Blackpool' history lesson with her Year 5 class.

Aly: *I knew the children pretty well as it was coming up to the end of my six-week placement. They had got really excited about learning about their town, Blackpool, during the Victorian era. We'd learned a lot together, actually, about the impact of the electric light and how that had led to the Blackpool illuminations that still happen and attract thousands of tourists every year. I'd developed lots of links between subjects, like electrical circuits in science, and designing lights in D&T. We'd also looked at how the growth of the railway had brought all those tourists into Blackpool and how Blackpool had grown because of it. I wanted another way of bringing all this learning together so they could see the growth of the town for themselves, including when their own streets and the town familiar to them formed.*

I just Googled 'archive map Blackpool' or something like that and I got loads more than I expected. Then I did the same for 'population'. I printed all the details out and intentionally made sure that there were gaps in the information, like some of the maps didn't have dates. I presented all the data to the children and asked them to see if they could put some chronological order on all the data I'd thrown at them. They had to use books of local history I had from the school library service and some I'd borrowed from the uni library. There were photos I'd copied, with the names of streets that they had to find on maps.

Interviewer: *How did it go?*

Aly: *Well, that was the amazing thing! They did just get on and do it! They loved it! It made the whole thing come alive for them. Obviously a lot of them are from families who have several generations in Blackpool. For example, the twins were interested to find the approximate date the road their Granddad's place of work was built. I never dreamt that using so many different sources of data, you know, the archive census lists, the maps, the population graphs, the tourist information figures, the photos, the books ... just how all of it could have been so interesting to them.*

Interviewer: *So what have you learnt from that lesson?*

Aly: *Oh wow, well ... using a range of data sources is enriching for the children, and getting them to solve a problem by giving them some but not all of the data. That seemed to clinch it for their interest. I've never seen so many bottoms in the air and heads down low together on the carpet for such a long duration like that! Their class teacher said she hadn't seen them behave like that either. I do have to tell you about Jared though.*

$\rightarrow$

Interviewer: *Oh yes?*

Aly: *He was funny. As they were going out for their lunch, he said to his friend, but really loudly so I could hear, 'I really hated that lesson.' So, of course I took the bait and asked him why he didn't like it. Do you know what he said? He said because it made him think! Ha ha, that's the best reason I've ever heard to hate a lesson. He is one of the children who I'd say is one of the higher-attaining children in the class. Of course it wouldn't be cool to say he enjoyed it, but I think that it was his way of telling me he liked it. I'm glad it made him think. That made my day.*

Do you recall the earlier research focus outlining Molinero and García-Madruga's research revealing that children ask more questions the more they know about a topic? The 'gap factor' they identified can be observed in the case study. Also in line with Molinero and García-Madruga's research, the children were motivated to use the data they were presented with because they were asking the questions. They used a number of mathematical skills during the history lesson, which are outlined below.

Analysing data

During this chapter we have highlighted the importance of making data meaningful for children in order to offer contexts that motivate them. Ainley (2000, page 371) demonstrates that using meaningful data meant that children *could intuitively make sense of it even when they had not collected the data themselves: the experience of having [a meaningful context] was … enough for them to be able to make it ready at hand in making sense of the data.* Making sense of the data that are available is important when analysing them.

In order to analyse most data sets, it is necessary to manipulate the data in some way so that they can be efficiently and effectively analysed. The most common methods used are construction and interpretation of graphs. du Feu (2008, page 2) gives us food for thought when explaining that *the implication [of the curriculum] is that both construction and reading a given type of chart are of equal intellectual demand. The consequence – which can be seen in typical schemes of work and textbooks – is that these two aspects are often taught together.* du Feu explains that because the main function of statistical diagrams is to *communicate information in a way that is easy to assimilate,* constructing graphs may be more challenging than interpreting them. This can be seen in the case study above, where the children were able to use complex sources of data to ask questions and answer them, but certainly would not have been able to create the data in the way they were presented to them in one morning.

Using ICT to support the analysis of data

Activity

Reflect on a lesson you have observed or taught that involved creating graphs and answer the following questions.

- What was the purpose of the graphs?
- What was the purpose of the children constructing the graphs?
- Did the children construct the graphs by hand or did they use technology to construct the graph for them?
- What would have been in the implications for the learning outcomes if the children had constructed the graphs the other way, either by using technology or by hand?
- What did the children do with the graphs once they were constructed? Did they use or apply them in any way, or were they an end product in their own right?

We would like to argue that very rarely should you be planning for children to construct graphs by hand as a means to an end in a lesson. Although children are required to be able to construct graphs, using technology to do this makes effective use of ICT by reducing the amount of tedious construction children need to do. Normally, the purpose of constructing a graph will be to create a tool for analysing data or as a means to communicate findings to an audience, as part of a process that involves using and applying handling data knowledge, skills and understanding.

Links to the National Curriculum

Nowhere in the National Curriculum are children required to construct graphs by hand. When children are processing, representing and interpreting data, they are expected to be able to construct tables and graphs (Ma4 2b) but the method of construction is not stipulated. Indeed, in using and applying handling data (Ma4 1) children are expected to be able to *approach problems flexibly, including trying alternative approaches to overcome any difficulties* (Ma4 1b), and *decide how to best organise and present findings* (Ma4 1f).

Using a computer to construct graphs that can easily and quickly be changed uses the affordances that ICT gives us to enable children to learn these problem solving and communicating skills appropriately (Ainley, 2000; Ainley *et al.*, 2001).

To summarise, when children are collecting their own primary data, you have the crucial role in ensuring they use the most appropriate method of collection so that their work is not wasted. Be aware of the time that collecting data takes. If your objective is not related to data collection, look at whether or not secondary data are a more sensible option for the children to collect or for you to present to them. Analysis of data must also be carried out so that the original question or problem is answered.

Presenting and reflecting on findings

Tresidder (2006, page 44) explores the need for children to understand how data *are used and how to interpret them. The ability to be critical and sceptical is particularly important in assessing statistical information.* The types of teaching methods we are suggesting in this book *present great opportunities for cross-curricular exploration and for teachers to be able to demonstrate the power and relevance of mathematics outside the classroom.* She goes on to warn that *we become so absorbed with working out how we can help [the children] to meet the various marking criteria that we lose sight of the bigger picture – of turning out citizens that can make sense of and critically evaluate statistics presented to them in the everyday world.*

Data are so much part of our lives now that we see them presented to us almost constantly. For example, we can drive along a road and see a sign that tells us the number of serious injuries or fatalities that have occurred on that section in a given period. When entering a town or village an electronic sign flashes your current speed, reminding you to slow down. They even appear to us on personal objects such as a Nintendo Wii Fit to provide our latest weight or body mass index. Medication provides statistics related to the number of patients through trials that had certain side effects. While those data may be correct, there are many other sources that could, at best, be misleading and, at worst, downright wrong. Advertisements selling the latest model of car or beauty product also use data presented in various ways to encourage us to buy them. Figures and graphs are presented in news articles. These should not be taken at face value – you will be familiar with the adage 'lies, damned lies and statistics'.

Presenting data

> *I find it deeply worrying that numbers are trusted so completely. Text is no longer believed at face value: we ask who wrote it, who commissioned it, who might benefit from it, etc. We know that people write to persuade and convince. Digits seem to get away scot-free! The meaning behind a CATS or contextual value added score or a Fisher Family Trust prediction is assumed to be clear and uncontested. There is no suggestion that these numbers come with any margin of error or that there might be anything suspect in the process that produces them.*

> (Edmunds, 2006)

Therefore, understanding how data are presented is a crucial element of a primary child's mathematical learning. The research below demonstrates that teachers may tend to overlook this, leading to poorer outcomes of children's attainment in the areas identified.

Research Focus

In their analyses of the 2002, 2003 and 2004 statutory tests, the Qualification and Curriculum Authority found that for Key Stage 1, teachers needed to:

- encourage children to think about the whole set of data presented in bar graphs by asking questions such as, 'How many children does the graph show were in the class?';

- encourage children to interpret scales accurately;

- provide more experience to children to use two-criteria Carroll diagrams so that children were able to sort and describe the objects in each region by relating them to the criteria for that region as well as explaining why objects do not belong to a particular subset.

The Key Stage 2 analyses identified similar issues. The implications for teaching and learning were that teachers needed to:

- teach children strategies for reading scales on graphs calibrated in different ways;

- teach children strategies for reading graphs accurately, including identifying the values that lay between labelled increments;

- present children with data presented in a wide range of tables and charts to give them more experience of interpreting data.

Similar issues arose in all three reports and again in a report from the National Strategies (2009), providing a strong evidence base to suggest that these are clearly aspects that teachers must pay more attention to in their planning and teaching.

The following case study illustrates how one trainee teacher used Carroll diagrams with Year 1. Notice how his science planning used data presented in ways that were new to the children. This reflects the trainee's high expectations of the children.

Case Study: Floating and sinking

Martin was on a one-week placement that was focusing specifically on scientific thinking. The topic that his class teacher had asked him to use was 'floating and sinking'. The previous day the children had stayed together on the carpet and recorded their hypotheses about which objects might float and sink. The discussion had developed to focus on the impact the size of a shape will have on its ability to float or sink.

Martin says, *I noticed that over the time on the carpet some of the children had ideas in their heads that were obvious misconceptions. One common one was that*

$\rightarrow$

'big objects sink and small objects float'. Another one was that metal objects sink. I laughed to myself because I thought, 'they haven't thought about the big ocean liners, have they?'

So I developed this sheet [see Figure 5.4] using a Carroll diagram to help them to see that size does not define whether an object can float. Some of the children found the two criteria difficult to get their heads around. I wasn't surprised as they aren't expected to know it till the end of next year. But I put them in mixed-attainment groups according to their maths attainment to try and balance that out. I also made sure there was a confident writer in each group too. It worked out pretty well, especially because there was a lot of discussion in each group about where to place each object on the diagram. The adults were there to support as and when. I was a little worried about water and children working in groups, but the children stayed focused on the task in hand.

FLOATING AND SINKING CARROLL DIAGRAM

	Floats	~~Floats~~
Large	botul tinfoil wud	Sunglasis mug
~~Large~~	beads Pensul Pompom cork	cLip roola

Figure 5.4 Floating and sinking Carroll diagram record sheet

Reflecting upon the findings

Chapter 1 explained how humans are natural problem-solvers. Given the data-rich environment that we now live in, it is important that you encourage children to reflect on what they have found out in order to draw together the data-handling process to ensure that they are indeed solving the initial problem they were setting out to solve. To do this, the children will also be drawing on the other using and applying skills of reasoning and communication. Reflecting upon the findings includes the children:

- discussing the findings;
- using their intuition to decide on its applicability;
- analysis of the graphs;

- using metacognition to evaluate the effectiveness of their findings and the process they followed.

Research Focus: Metacognition as a tool for reflection

Desoete (2009) explains how some children find dealing with information processing and problem-solving difficult. She presents an argument that metacognition skills may be less developed for these children. She explains how metacognition can be defined as *the knowledge, awareness, and deeper understanding of one's own cognitive processes and products* and how it can be used as a variable to *differentiate children with learning disabilities from below-average performing children and average performers from expert problem-solvers* (page 436).

In her research, Desoete worked over a two-year period with 66 Grade 3 children in Belgium where she developed children's metacognitive and evaluative skills. Desoete's research presents an argument for explicitly teaching metacognition and evaluation in order to *develop and enhance mathematical problem-solving skills* (page 436).

We suggest that reflecting on findings and on the process undertaken is a worthwhile mechanism to teach metacognitive skills to children.

To summarise, presenting and reflecting on findings significantly uses reasoning, communicating and problem-solving skills. The presentation and reflection on findings should not necessarily be seen at the outset as the end-point of a data-handling cycle. Indeed, this part of the process may in fact bring up additional issues that need to be explored, or may reveal that the process has not brought about a conclusion at this stage.

Learning Outcomes Review

This chapter has explained how handling data is a relatively recently introduced mathematical notion, but how it is essential to be able to use and apply it in today's society. We have tried to challenge your notion of what data might look like, by suggesting that data include maps, for example. The chapter developed how problem-solving, reasoning and communication skills are used in the learning of handling data from a mathematical perspective and how data handling can aid the learning of other subject areas.

Self-assessment questions

1. The introduction of this chapter asked you to keep Articles 12 and 14 from the United Nations Convention on the Rights of the Child (UNCRC) in your mind as you read this chapter. How to you think the knowledge, skills and

understanding that are developed through handling data empower children to enact this right?

2. Why is the data-handling process seen as a cycle, rather than as a linear process?

3. Using ICT can empower children to analyse data. Make a list of the affordances that ICT offers over manipulating data by hand.

Further Reading

There are two chapters in this book that explore further the use and application of data – see Chapters 7 and 8.

Brown, S.I. and Walter, M.I. (2005) *The art of problem posing*. Hillsdale, NJ: Lawrence Erlbaum Associates Ltd. This encourages you to think about where problems come from and how to incorporate problem posing into your mathematics teaching.

Cohen, L., Manion, L. and Morrison, K. (2011) *Research methods in education*. London: Routledge. This explores in great depth all the methods of data collection you or your children will use.

Metcalfe, J. and Simpson, D. (2011) Learning online: The internet, social networking and e-safety. Chapter 6 in Simpson, D. and Toyn, M. (eds) *Primary ICT across the curriculum* alerts you to be able to: identify risks associated with children's use of new technologies; be aware of the range of ways that schools and teachers can contribute to children's safe use of new technologies both in and outside of educational settings; and recognise ways in which social and learning networks can support children's learning across the curriculum.

Mooney, C., Hansen, A., Wrathmell, R., Fox, S. and Ferrie, L. (2011) Handling data and probability, in Mooney *et al. Primary mathematics: Knowledge and understanding*. This explains how to choose the best method of collecting, recording, representing and interpreting data, as well as how to find the mean, median, mode and range and understand when best to use them (see Chapter 6). Chapter 12 goes on to explain how to present data and how to use ICT effectively in handling data.

References

Ainley, J. (2000) Transparency in graphs and graphing tasks: An iterative design process. *Journal of Mathematical Behavior*, 19: 365–384.

Ainley, J., Pratt, D. and Nardi, E. (2001) Normalising: Children's activity to construct meanings for trend. *Educational Studies in Mathematics*, 35: 131–146.

Allen, G.A. (1997) The origins of mathematics. *The History of Mathematics*. Spring, 1997. Available at **www.math.tamu.edu/~dallen/history/origins/origins.html** (accessed 20/11/10).

Collins, G.P. (2002) Claude E. Shannon: Founder of information theory. *Scientific American*, 14 October, 2002. Available at **www.scientificamerican.com/article.cfm?id=claude-e-shannon-founder** (accessed 20/11/10).

du Feu, C. (2008) Using statistics for teaching primary school children. *Teaching Statistics*, 30 (1): 2–5.

Edmunds, F. (2006) Handling the data. *Mathematics teaching incorporating micromath*, 196: 47.

Frazier, B.N., Gelman, S.A. and Wellman, H.M. (2009) Preschoolers' search for explanatory information within adult-child conversation. *Child Development*, 80 (6): 1592–1611.

Funkhouser, H.G. (1937) Historical development of the graphical representation of statistical data. *Osiris*, 3. (1937): 269–404.

Holmes, P. (2003) 50 years of statistics teaching in English schools: Some milestones. *The Statistician*, 52 (4): 439–474.

Molinero, R.I. and García-Madruga, J.A. (2011) Knowledge and question asking. *Psicothema*, 23 (1): 26–30.

National College (2011) Student voice. Available at **www.nationalcollege.org.uk/index/leadershiplibrary/leadingschools/ecm/school-families-communities/student-voice.htm** (accessed 25/2/11).

Office for National Statistics (2001) **www.statistics.gov.uk/census2001/bicentenary/history.html** (accessed 3/5/11).

Tresidder, G. (2006) Data handling and citizenship. *Mathematics Teaching incorporating Micromath*, 197: 40–44.

UNCRC (1989) Convention on the Rights of the Child. Office of the United Nations High Commissioner for Human Rights. Available at **http://www2.ohchr.org/english/law/crc.htm** (accessed 8/3/11).

PART 2
USING MATHEMATICS IN YOUR WIDER PROFESSIONAL ROLE

6. Using mathematics to support the organisation of learning and teaching

Learning Outcomes

The chapter explores how mathematics helps you to organise:
- the learning environment;
- class trips;
- sports days and other games;
- the timetable;
- the budget for your classroom;
- your cross-curricular planning.

Professional Standards for QTS

Q3 (a) Be aware of the professional duties of teachers and the statutory framework within which they work.

Q7 (b) Identify priorities for their early professional development in the context of induction.

Q8 Have a creative and constructively critical approach towards innovation, being prepared to adapt their practice where benefits and improvements are identified.

Q14 Have a secure knowledge and understanding of their subjects/curriculum areas and related pedagogy to enable them to teach effectively across the age and ability range for which they are trained.

Q29 Evaluate the impact of their teaching on the progress of all learners, and modify their planning and classroom practice where necessary.

Q30 Establish a purposeful and safe learning environment conducive to learning and identify opportunities for learners to learn in out-of-school contexts.

Introduction

In Part 1 of this book we discussed the need for children to be able to reason, problem-solve and communicate. You also need to use these skills both as a trainee and a qualified teacher. Before you qualify you will be expected to pass the QTS numeracy skills test. This will test your own knowledge of mathematics at a level that is beyond that expected to be able to teach primary children. It will involve questions that test your knowledge of mathematics that would be required to undertake professional duties as outlined in Chapter 7, such as analysis of school data, interpretation of box and whisker diagrams and much more. These questions will test your own ability to reason, problem-solve and communicate. See the Further Reading section for where to go for further guidance and support on this QTS numeracy skills test.

Through case studies and activities this chapter will help you to understand the mathematical knowledge involved in such things as organising the learning environment, creating a workable classroom timetable, ordering stock for your classroom, organising a school trip and much more.

Organising the learning environment

As a trainee teacher you will have worked in classrooms with different layouts. Have you stopped to think why furniture and resources are placed where they are? Have you observed teachers or been involved in moving the furniture around so that the learning environment is fit for purpose? One of the things that you will need to think about once you become a teacher or during your placements is the design of your classroom. If you are going to make the most effective use of the available space you will need to arrange the furniture and resources to provide a learning environment that is safe and allows for the minimum alteration in order to deliver the maximum learning opportunities. As you will see later in this chapter when thinking about the timetable, time is at a premium and you do not want children to be spending valuable learning time moving and reorganising furniture.

How often have you decided to move an entire room of furniture around at home only to discover that the very reason you have it a certain way is because that is the only way it will all fit in? In school this can sometimes be the case too. You may have to accept that pedagogically you would like a certain learning environment but realistically you have to settle for what fits. Placement of resources is also crucial and where a teacher chooses to place particular resources often reflects aspects of their own philosophy of education.

In Chapter 3 we discussed ways of teaching area and perimeter and shared the case study 'A new garden'. In the same way, you will need to be able to design your classroom. Unlike Daniel and his class, who were able to start from scratch, you will have to use the resources and equipment that already exist. If you do have the opportunity to do this with the children it can be a very effective way of combining your reasoning, problem-solving and communicating skills with theirs. After all, they are going to be using the classroom from a different perspective to you and so may have some excellent ideas of their own.

Activity

This activity gives you an opportunity for you to design your ideal classroom for a class of 34 children. Two children have hearing difficulties and another will be on crutches for most of the Autumn term. Make a list of the things you will need to consider for these children. For example, you might need to consider the space between the desks, the distance of the desks from the board, and so on.

Below is the beginning of a list of the basic requirements for any classroom to function, with room left for you to add more items. In Chapter 2 we discussed the need for children to be able to understand number and the assumptions that we make about prior knowledge. We ask children to estimate the length of a table or the height of a chair during tasks in mathematics lessons. In just the same way we now ask you to complete the dimensions column before finding the actual measurements from either a school supplies website or catalogue, or by measuring some furniture in a classroom.

Type of furniture	Dimensions
Children's tables	
Children's chairs	
Teacher's table	
Teacher's chair	
Resources cupboards –	
Trolley with plastic trays for children	
Class library area	
Other display areas	
Other	

Now create a scale diagram of the classroom, including the position of the items, from the list above. You must also remember that there will be a door and windows and you will need to indicate where the children mentioned at the start of the activity will be sitting.

While completing the first part of this activity, did you struggle to add dimensions? Why would you know the height of a chair? How did you decide on the size of the classroom? Did you measure an actual room or did you arrange the furniture and then see how big the room needed to be? Furniture showrooms often display their furniture as if it were in rooms in a house. Has this ever caught you out? Often the dimensions of the 'rooms' on display are larger than those in regular houses. Furniture salespeople always check that the dimensions of new large furniture, such as sofas, will actually fit into your house. This is because the large showroom can be deceptive to customers.

In Chapter 4 we asked you to consider why children find it difficult to estimate measures. How are children meant to comprehend any quantity if they have no baseline to work from? If you know how tall you are and you are asked the height of someone who is taller than you, then you have the starting point of your own height. If children are given the opportunity to compare and contrast units of measure and numeric value then they will be able to begin to think in the abstract. If they know that a fizzy drinks bottle holds two litres of liquid, when presented with questions in such things as SATs like: 'How much water does a bath hold?' they will have a mental picture to work from.

In the second part of the activity did you consider group work, practical lessons, access to water, paint, etc.? When you are next on placement, take time to observe different room layouts. Ask teachers to explain the reasons for these and begin to think how your ideal classroom would look.

For more detailed information about how the Disability Discrimination Act should be implemented in schools, see Further Reading.

Planning educational visits

In Chapter 2 we discussed how mathematics trails are a useful opportunity for learning outside the classroom. This section looks more broadly at educational visits which can range from an hour to a whole week. Regardless of their length, all necessitate a great deal of forward planning to ensure that they most effectively address the curriculum objectives and fit appropriately within the school year.

A visit to a local museum can bring the history curriculum to life. Most museums have education rooms and staff who are able to plan activities for your class. Children get the opportunity to handle objects and artefacts that ordinarily would be locked in display cabinets (Coughlin, 2010). In Chapter 2, the case study 'Egypt', identified how Year 3 children were given the task of planning a trip to Egypt. A visit to the local travel agent to collect holiday brochures and talk to the staff brings this kind of activity to life. Many of the larger supermarkets also have education rooms and staff employed to liaise with local schools. They are keen to invite schoolchildren in to the store to learn about the running of their business. For Key Stage 1 children a simple walk to the local post office to collect items for their role-play area offers them the chance to observe the layout of the real thing and ask questions. Of course you cannot turn up with 34 Year 1 children at the local post office! All class trips take meticulous planning and organisation.

Ideally any educational visit should enhance the work being carried out inside the classroom. See Chapter 4's case study 'The recycling centre' for an illustration of how a trainee teacher used a pre-trip visit to help him plan the children's learning within the classroom. Another powerful way to extend the types of trips mentioned above is to create with the children a role-play area in the classroom (Briggs and Hansen, in press). See discussion about role-play in Chapter 2 as a way to extend mathematics trails also.

Activity

Reflect on an educational visit that you have attended as a trainee teacher, or as a pupil. What did the experience add to the children's learning?

The following research focus presents some advantages to and practical advice for planning educational visits.

Research Focus

Many teachers and schools organise class trips. Noel (2007, page 43) reminds us that *learning is optimized only when teachers actively integrate the content of the field trip with the curriculum*. In her research that focused on collaborating between stakeholders to provide meaningful learning experiences for children, Coughlin (2010) describes how a historical society, university professor and local school district (in the USA) provided Grade 3 children a practical experience for learning about historical research, a historical schoolhouse and chronology. She found that school trips generally:

- provide a *lived learning* experience, connecting with first-hand experience;
- linked children's learning to a particular place, person or object;
- increase collaboration between children and teachers;
- can be inexpensive;
- can help children to explore 'powerful ideas' (such as 'change');
- offer hands-on activities that enable children to recall information;
- offer high-quality learning resources.

She also noted that school trips require careful planning and collaboration. Planning should allow:

- flexible integration of curriculum subjects;
- for close co-operation with site co-ordinators to ensure participation and discussion;
- age-related interests and capabilities;
- appropriate pre- and post-visit activities.

The cost of any school trip can be the deciding factor as to whether it actually goes ahead or not. Although children are entitled to free school education for activities offered wholly or mainly during the normal teaching time, schools are able to charge for optional activities provided wholly or mainly out of school hours. For some parents this can be a heavy burden and so careful thought has to go into the reason for the trip. Each school governing body will have written a policy outlining what their school's decisions are on these charges. Within later block placements you may be asked to plan a trip for the class and it will be necessary for you to be able to work out the cost of the trip from start to finish in line with the particular guidelines for that school.

Furthermore, there are other considerations that involve mathematical skills beyond those of budgeting. For example, the health and safety of the children is paramount and risk assessments must be carried out. In this excerpt from the DfEE it is possible to see an application for ratio.

> Some LEAs set their own levels of supervision for off-site visits, which county and controlled schools must adhere to. In other schools decisions must be made, taking the above factors into consideration as part of the risk assessment. Staffing ratios for visits are difficult to prescribe as they will vary according to the activity, age, group, location and the efficient use of resources. However, a general guide for visits to local historical sites and museums or for local walks, in normal circumstances, might be:
>
> - 1 adult for every 6 pupils in school years 1 to 3 (under 5s reception classes should have a higher ratio);
> - 1 adult for every 10–15 pupils in school years 4 to 6;
> - 1 adult for every 15–20 pupils in school year 7 onwards.
>
> The above are examples only. Group leaders should assess the risks and consider an appropriate safe supervision level for their particular group. There should be a minimum of one teacher in charge.
>
> In addition to the teacher in charge there should be enough supervisors to cope effectively with an emergency. When visits are to remote areas or involve hazardous activities, the risks may be greater and supervision levels should be set accordingly. The same consideration should be given to visits abroad or residential visits. Some non-residential visits with mixed groups will need a teacher from each sex.
>
> (DfEE, 1998)

Activity

One of the governors of your placement school is the local constituency MP. She has been into school and worked closely with the Year 6 class to explain her role and how she has to be in Parliament for part of the time. She has invited the class to London to visit her in her office and to be shown around the Houses of Parliament. It has been decided to combine this with a visit to other London attractions and take the children away for a week.

The list below gives just some of the many things that will need to be organised for this trip that involve mathematics in some way.

- Liaison with the MP regarding a mutually agreeable date.
- Costing of the complete trip and informing the parents.
- Arranging adequate adult supervision and ensuring CRB checks have been carried out.
- Train times and cost.
- Hotels – how many rooms, allocation of rooms.
- Distance of hotel from activities.
- Opening times of attractions.
- Timetable for the week.
- Size of groups.

The head teacher has asked you to be responsible for working out how much it will cost to take the class of 34 on the train. She wants to know the cheapest option with times and dates. Using the DfEE guidelines given above, choose a departure point and complete this activity for a Year 6 class. Compile an itinerary to give to the head teacher.

How did you begin the activity? Did you make a list of numbers, ages, times, etc.? Did you use the internet to input data and let it work it out for you or did you do the calculations yourself using a paper copy of train times and ticket prices? Perhaps you thought that a coach might be more cost effective as then you would have it in London for the week.

This activity is just a small part of the process and complex work that is involved in taking children out of school. However, if you are going to help children make the link between what they learn in school and the world around them then it is essential that you use opportunities such as the one in the activity.

Games lessons and sports day

Earlier in this chapter you were asked to begin to think about the mathematics involved in organising and designing your own classroom. In Chapter 2 the case study: 'Maths trails in Year 2', gave an example of setting a mathematics trail in the local town. In this next section we once again consider the outside environment and begin to think of the mathematics involved in utilising this available space in much the same way. Haigh (2009) identifies some examples of how mathematics is used in sport, including scoring systems in motor racing and tennis, league tables in chess and football, statistical phenomena in basketball and golf, as well as batting averages in cricket. Many primary schools have playing fields that act as football pitches, rounders pitches, running tracks and of course playgrounds and in your teaching career you may well be in the position of being responsible for setting out some sort of games provision area.

Activity

Imagine you want to take your class out to play rounders. The school has a fairly large playing field but you need to make sure that there is sufficient room for a game to be played. As it is some time since any class has played rounders, there is no marked pitch, but there is a diagram (see Figure 6.1) in the PE co-ordinator's file in the staff room.

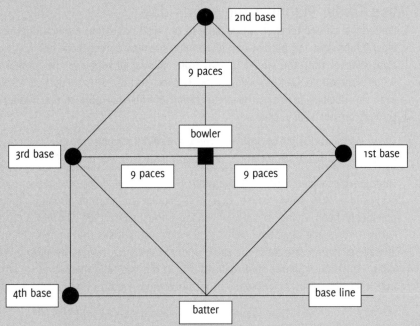

Figure 6.1 The dimensions of a rounders pitch

Having looked at the diagram, work out the exact measurements in metric units and create a new diagram. You will need to know that a pace is equivalent to 30 inches. Now answer the following questions.

- What would be the minimum area that you need on the field?
- What would be the maximum area that you need on the field?
- How far away from the school building will the pitch need to be?

Now that you have completed this, look back at your diagram and your answers.

Did you consider:

- any health and safety requirements?

- the distance a child can hit a ball?

- the direction the ball will go when hit?

- the orientation of the pitch?

Even if you are not involved in planning where the different pitches and tracks are positioned, it is very likely that you will be involved in the yearly event of sports day and the mathematics involved in this event at some stage during your training. You will need to organise your class in the preceding weeks with practice races, teams and relays. On the day you may be in charge of a stop watch at the finish of the race and be expected to rank the children as they finish each race.

Case Study: Planning the sports day

Emma is a trainee teacher specialising in physical education undertaking her final block placement. As part of her placement she has agreed with her mentor and class teacher that she would benefit from helping to organise the annual inter-school football competition held at her school. Because it is a Football World Cup year she decides to make the organisation of this day part of the mathematics content for her Year 6 class.

She gives them this initial problem: There are seven schools and each school needs to play every other school once. How many matches will this be?

Through discussion and collaboration the children begin to come up with suggestions and soon realise that it is similar to another problem they had previously been trying to solve involving handshakes. (See Chapter 1 Research Focus 'Developing reasoning skills' to see how using tasks that appear different in 'surface structure' but have the same underlying structure may develop reasoning skills.) Once the children had realised this, it did not take them long to work out that if all the teams played each other once there would need to be 21 matches.

> We worked out that team **a** played the 6 other teams once so that is 6 games. Then team **b** played the other teams but that wouldn't me 6 times cos they have already played team a so we took off that game which meant team **b** played 5 games. Then team **c** played all their games but they had already played b and a so that was only 4 games. Then team **d** played their ones but they had already done it against c b a so it was 3 games. Then we saw the pattern like this:
>
> Team a = 6 games
>
> Team b = 5 games
>
> Team c = 4 games
>
> Team d = 3 games
>
> Team e = 2 games
>
> Team f = 1 game
>
> It went down each time. So we added all the games together and it was ...
>
> **21 games!**
>
> Isaac, Spencer, Dillon, Jay

Figure 6.2 Solution 1

$\longrightarrow$

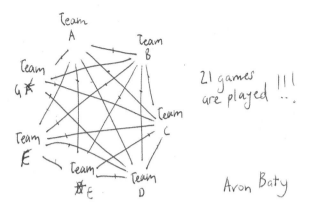

21 games
are played !!!

Avon Baty

Figure 6.3 Solution 2

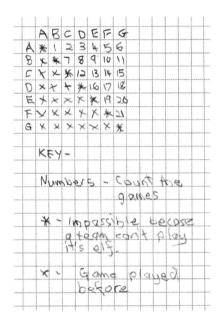

Figure 6.4 Solution 3

She was pleased that they had recognised the link between the problems and encouraged the more able children to see if they could produce a formula for any amount of teams, which would be really useful just in case one of the teams dropped out and they had to rearrange the day. It was not long before one of the children pointed out that the numbers involved were triangular numbers and gave the formula.

Emma and the class then went on to work out how many pitches they could fit on to the field, what time the day needed to start/end, how much juice they needed to buy. The children were then involved in the running of the event.

Clearly Emma was confident in her own mathematical subject knowledge and able to work with the more able children in the class. In fact several weeks' work was involved in this application of mathematical knowledge and ability to a real problem with a successful conclusion. Not only was Emma able to use her own mathematical knowledge and skills but she was also able to assess the knowledge of the children in a very practical way from the ideas they had and the results they produced.

Links to the National Curriculum

Being involved in the organisation and running of the sports event the children were able to use many skills required for both mathematics and PE. In order to work out the initial problem of how many games would be played, children had to collaborate, reason and problem-solve (Ma 1b break down a more complex problem into simpler steps before attempting a solution, 1f organise work and refine ways of working, 4d recognise, represent and interpret simple number relationships, constructing and using formulae in words then symbols). Within PE children are required to work with others taking part in designing challenges and competitions (10a, 11c).

Research Focus

Trudeau and Shephard (2008) undertook a significant literature review that looked at physical education, school physical activity, school sports and academic performance. They identified several research projects that explored the relationship between the amount of physical activity (PE, sports or other physical activity) and academic performance.

They found several instances where increased physical activity or physical education had a positive impact on children's mathematical or arithmetical attainment. This was also the case when time was taken from mathematical lessons for PE. Furthermore, Trudeau and Shephard identified that children were more likely to increase their attachment to school and self-esteem. These, although more indirect findings, also contribute to academic achievement.

The findings from the review in the research focus above raise questions about organising the timetable, an aspect of a teacher's role that we now turn to.

Organising the timetable

When you are a trainee teacher you will probably work from a class timetable given to you and so may not be aware of the time that it has taken to produce this in order that all subjects are given the appropriate amount of time throughout the year. However, it is important that you are aware of the time and effort that does go into timetabling in order for you to appreciate the school day when you are on placement. The more placement experiences you have, the more you will realise that there is no set pattern to the length of the school day. Some schools start at 8.30 a.m. and finish at 2.30 p.m. whilst others will start at 9 a.m. and finish at 3.30 p.m. Key Stage 1 and 2 often have different break times and lengths of break. Hall times for PE, allotted time for using such things as the ICT suite, going to swimming lessons, and slots for MFL are all things that are usually set as immovable times from the start of the year by the senior management. Some children may also be withdrawn for additional support as the other adults' timetable allows (Wedell *et al.*, 2008). At times external factors (such as a visiting theatre group or another teacher needing to swap sessions one week) will require a change in the timetable. At the beginning of this chapter we outlined some of the advantages of taking children on out-of-class trips and how these would need to be fitted into the timetable to ensure curriculum coverage is maintained. All these things can lead to a logistical planning nightmare for the staff involved and this is something you will need to be sensitive to on placement. You will need to be flexible to these needs, as your placement requirements (see Chapter 8 for an example) may also require changes. You will need to be sensitive to the needs of the school alongside your own.

Hours per subject

With all the change to the timetable that can occur during the school year, many teachers worry that subjects are not being given the correct amount of time. When a cross-curricular approach is used, a concern of teachers and parents can be that children are not getting the basic facts and that subject content is being lost as subjects are merged and children spend more time outside the classroom.

Although there are no statutory requirements for time allocated to subjects, schools must open for 380 half-day sessions (190 days) in each school year (**www.teachernet.gov.uk/ management/atoz/l/lengthofschoolday/**). The school year runs from September to July but in this time there are half terms, Christmas, Easter and Bank Holidays. Therefore if we take an average day as 9 a.m.–3.30 p.m. this would give us a maximum of 6.5 hours. However, the actual time for 'formal' lessons needs to be calculated by taking off such things as registration, assembly, morning break, lunch and afternoon break, which usually account for up to two hours, resulting in a time of 4.5 hours per day or 22.5 hours a week. The suggested minimum hours of learning are 21 for 5–7 year olds and 23.5 for 8–11 year olds. Clearly our 'average' day would seem to suggest that we have allowed too much time for Key Stage 1 but not enough for Key Stage 2 and as yet we have not even mentioned time for Christmas parties, plays, swimming, school trips, etc.

All subjects should be included over the year but there is no legal requirement for all foundation subjects to be taught every week, or even every term. However, guidance given to schools (QCDA, 2002) would suggest the breakdown of hours per subject per week (listed in Table 6.1). As you will notice, once the percentages have been rounded there would appear to be some flexibility to adjust certain subjects in each key stage such as science, PE and RE.

Subject	KS1 % of 21 hrs	KS1 Actual hours	KS2 % of 23.5hrs	KS2 Actual hours
English	36	8	32	8
Mathematics	18	4	21	5
Science	7	1	9	2
ICT	4	1	4	1
D&T	4	1	4	1
History	4	1	4	1
Geography	4	1	4	1
Art	4	1	4	1
Music	4	1	4	1
PE	6	1	5	1
RE	5	1	5	1
MFL	0		4	1
Total		20		23

Table 6.1 Guidance for time spent teaching curriculum subjects (QCDA, 2002)

As you can imagine, this is quite a task and does take up considerable time in school to get it correct and to the satisfaction of the governing body as any changes such as lengthening or shortening the school day need to be approved by them. What may seem like minor changes can have a tremendous knock-on effect. Adding or shortening the school day by half an hour may affect parents'/carers' child care provision, bus timetables taking children home, taxi companies dropping off and picking up children, to name but a few.

When you become a class teacher you may be asked to complete your own timetable and you will need to be mindful of the figures discussed above.

Activity

Using the suggested time per subject above, try to complete the weekly timetable given below for a Year 6 class.

You will notice that some things have already been set such as assembly, break, lunch, PE, ICT and modern foreign languages because, as has been previously mentioned, these are usually things that are decided as a whole school.

Day	9.00–9.30	9.30–10.30	10.30–10.45	10.45–12.00	12.00–1.00	1.00–2.00	2.00–2.15	2.15–3.15
Mon	Registration Assembly					MFL		
Tues	Registration Assembly			ICT suite				
Wed	Registration Assembly		BREAK		LUNCH		BREAK	
Thurs	Registration Assembly			PE – Hall				
Fri	Registration Assembly							

Did you find that activity quite difficult to do? You may have decided that there just wasn't enough time to fit everything in.

Look again and try to change the times to fit exactly.

What would you alter?

How would you justify these alterations?

In Chapter 1 we mentioned the debate surrounding integrated and single-subject learning opportunities. Copping (2011) discusses this in further depth. The activity above might suggest that there is a strong case to support the need for a cross-curricular approach in order to ensure that all subjects are delivered appropriately. There is also a growing argument for more PE to be included within the week from the Healthy Schools agenda (**http://home.healthyschools. gov.uk/**). PSHE also needs to be considered and if setting across year groups is carried out across mathematics and English then this too will have an effect on where things are placed during the day.

It may have occurred to you that it is strange to be asked to complete the above activity of planning a timetable for discrete subjects within a book where the theme is taking a cross-curricular approach. Although a cross-curricular approach has been shown to be an effective pedagogy, it is only the case when you are still aware of the subject objectives of what is being taught so that you can maintain subject integrity in your teaching. So, the timetabling activity above was deliberate because it is in planning learning that you use a cross-curricular approach, not in planning a timetable.

We discuss how problem-solving, reasoning and communication are skills used in planning cross-curricular links in the section that follows.

Using mathematical skills when planning in cross-curricular ways

Up until this point we have been intentionally evasive about defining what we mean by a cross-curricular approach. The reason for this is that there are a number of interpretations and we do not want to constrain the different approaches that would be classed as cross-curricular. Regardless of the approach, they all share certain principles that you see reflected in this book. These principles are identified below.

The most significant reason for learning within a cross-curricular environment is that it pays the following dividends for the learners.

1. Children do not learn in compartments. Having discrete lessons labelled as particular 'subjects' sets up an artificial learning approach and presents a situation where there are unnecessary barriers to learning.

2. Children are creative, reflective learners. A cross-curricular approach gives more time for children to engender these life skills (Briggs and Hansen, in press).

3. Children learn key skills such as communication (Dannels and Housley-Gaffney, 2009). This is crucial. In an analysis of cross-curricular skills testing in the Netherlands, Meijer (2007, page 155) found that *cross-curricular skills appear to have more in common with academic achievement than with intelligence*, suggesting that if children master certain skills then they can access the content of curriculum more effectively.

Teaching using a cross-curricular approach pays dividends for the teacher because combining similar National Curriculum objectives from different subjects to teach together provides an opportunity to 'free up' other parts of the day. To see an example of the potential number of objectives that can be combined, see the National Curriculum links feature in Chapter 3. If even some of these were brought together, it would enable children to explore the objectives more deeply, or provide more time to teach other objectives more effectively.

Fogarty and Pete (2009) introduce a number of models of integrated approaches to learning. If you want to know more about these, refer to the Further Reading section at the end of this chapter.

Planning

There are many mathematical skills that you use when you are planning cross-curricular approaches. Often you will need to problem-solve by thinking about the time allocated to a unit of work and the objectives that you have identified you want to help the children achieve.

Making connections is something that you do when you are problem-solving; using reasoning and concept maps are a useful step in initial planning. They help you to make connections which support the development of meaningful links. What decisions will you make about which components to include and exclude? This uses your skills in data handling, making sense of all the information you have gathered and deciding on the best outcome (see Chapter 8 for further discussion).

Monitoring objectives being learned

Approaching learning and teaching in a cross-curricular way is very rewarding for the children and adults involved. A whole-school approach is the most effective form of delivery, facilitating collaborative planning across year groups linking objectives to the National Curriculum and key stages rather than a given year group. If for whatever reason you find that you are the only person in favour of this approach, it can work equally well within a single classroom. Of course a cross-curricular approach to learning requires excellent subject knowledge to ensure subject integrity but as the discussion above shows, the benefits are high.

We showed in Chapter 2 how some teaching you undertake may be spurred by chance questions from children, or other serendipitous circumstances. If using this method of teaching, then your planning of objectives and transferable skills needs to be carefully monitored, to ensure that you have addressed the National Curriculum objectives. Some teachers have access to software that helps them monitor and track the objectives used in their planning; other schools subscribe to creative curricula that provide detailed breakdowns of objectives the children are learning; and other teachers design their own checklists to ensure coverage over a term, year or key stage. This form of record-keeping is essential and the updating of the database is key for your accountability to your school management team (see Chapter 7 for how schools use data and about accountability), as well as creating a framework for your assessments records.

Budgeting

All schools have set budgets that they are required to keep detailed accounts of. These accounts are audited the same as any other business and it is the responsibility of the head teacher and school management team to ensure that money is spent wisely and not wasted. Monies are allocated to many different areas within the school. If in time you become a teacher governor involved in the finance committee then you will need to understand this allocation and make decisions about expenditure.

Control over school budget is something that NQTs in the USA identified as having little influence over (Liu, 2007). We suspect that these findings would be similar in Britain, but, as part of this overall budget will be the inclusion of classroom consumables, you will be responsible for ensuring sensible use of these when you are on placements. You may think a glue stick is an inexpensive consumable and not be too concerned if the top is left off and it dries up, but trust us, in any primary classroom this is a heinous act!

Each school decides how consumable goods will be ordered and distributed. Some allocate a certain amount of money per child and the class teacher has to spend this on things needed for the year, such as pens, paint, etc. When the goods arrive they are given to the class teacher and stored in the classroom to be used as needed throughout the year. Other schools pool the money and make one order for each key stage and others simply have one order for the whole school. In these cases resources are often stored in a central stock room.

Activity

Next time you are on placement, ask your placement mentor how your school manages classroom-based budgets for consumables. Also explore with your mentor how different teachers in the school manage their budget or resources.

Consider how you would manage the budget for your classroom, if you were an NQT in the school.

Case Study: A Key Stage 2 budget

Debbie is a deputy head teacher and new to the school. She is also the Key Stage 2 manager and a class teacher in Year 6.

On close inspection of the school's finances by the governors and the head teacher it has been noticed that a considerable amount of money is being spent each year on classroom consumables. In the past each class teacher had been responsible for producing their own order, handing it to the school administrator, taking delivery and storing things in their classroom stock cupboards. This has resulted in individual parcels being delivered from the same company at different times, incurring separate delivery charges that have mounted up and this now needs to be addressed.

In order to create a more effective ordering system, to avoid duplication, keep track of spending and to cut costs wherever possible, Debbie has been given overall responsibility to compile a list of consumables for the whole of the key stage ready for presenting to the senior management team before giving to the administrator to process.

The first thing she does is to make an inventory of all the existing stock that is stored across the key stage so that she can cross-match this to the orders from the individual teachers. A shared storage area is created and classroom cupboards emptied. Each teacher then compiles a list of their needs for the year with costings, and hands it to Debbie, who produces a spreadsheet showing actual expenditure with savings made through bulk buying or using existing stock and a prediction of expenditure for next year based on class numbers this year. She is also able to show expenditure per pupil across the key stage.

Once the list is approved by the school management team, all goods are ordered. The master list and individual class lists are sent to each teacher. On delivery, goods are first checked by the administrator and cross-referenced with payment documentation before being stored in the central storage area ready to be accessed by the class teachers when they are needed.

The result was:

- a more streamlined ordering system;
- a storage system that released valuable space in the classroom;
- no duplication of orders;
- a system for stocktaking before each new order;
- a reduction in the overall cost.

When you are a newly qualified teacher, you will find you have the responsibility of ordering equipment and resources for your class and this can be a very daunting experience. Do you know how much an exercise book costs? How many pencils will a child use each year? Are glue sticks really necessary?

Activity

Below is a list of some of the basic requirements for a primary school classroom. Imagine you are newly qualified and have been asked to compile an order for your new class of 34 Year 6 children.

Complete the quantity column and the estimated cost before accessing an educational resource catalogue, such as the one you used in the classroom equipment activity earlier in this chapter, to look up the actual cost.

Item	Quantity	Estimated cost	Actual cost
Pencils – drawing			
Crayons			
Felt pens			
Mathematics exercise books			
English exercise books			
A4 lined paper			
A4 plain white paper			
A3 drawing paper			
Glue sticks			
Writing pens			
Erasers			
Paint			
A4 coloured card			
Sugar paper			
	Total		

How close to the actual cost were you?
If you had to reduce the overall cost by 10 per cent what would you change in this list?

How did you begin to complete this activity? Were you tempted to go straight to the catalogue?

As a teacher you will expect the children to be able to estimate, and the importance of estimation is discussed in Chapter 4. Children need to have a baseline to work from, just as you will have done for the activity. You might have known how much a pencil or pen is as you will be buying them all the time for your own use, but what about an exercise book?

Did you think of the age of the children or the activities that they might be doing over the year as you completed the table? Do you think this order would be different for a Reception class and a Year 6 class?

Learning Outcomes Review

This chapter has explored the importance of trainee teachers being able to use mathematics effectively in all other aspects of the teacher's role. It has given as broad a range of examples as possible from arranging the furniture in your classroom to budgeting for resources for a complete school year. Throughout your teaching career you will be required to use and apply reasoning, problem-solving and communication skills to many different situations to effectively use mathematics in all other aspects of the teacher's role.

Self-assessment questions
1. The curriculum subjects that are required to be taught cannot fit into a school year if they are taught separately. How can teachers effectively meet the requirements of the National Curriculum, given that this is the case?
2. Provide at least five reasons for integrating out-of-school visits into your learning provision.
3. List some of the strategies that you have seen teachers using to ensure that class resources are not wasted.

Further Reading

DfES (2006) *Implementing the Disability Discrimination Act in Schools and Early Years Settings.* This is a boxed resource that your placement schools and provider library should have available for you to look at. Although aimed at head teachers, local authorities, schools and other voluntary child sectors, if you are interested in issues beyond those discussed in this chapter then this is a good place to start.

Fogarty, R.J. and Pete, B.M. (2009) *How to integrate the curricula.* Thousand Oaks, CA: Sage. This is a third edition of a book that discusses ten models for integrating curricula, noting the advantages and disadvantages of each as well as guidelines for implementing each model.

Patmore, M. (2008) *Passing the numeracy skills test.* Exeter: Learning Matters. This provides concise, practical help to prepare you for the QTS numeracy skills test.

TDA Skills Test (TDA) also provides guidance about the test. Visit **www.tda.gov.uk/trainee-teacher/qts-skills-tests/numeracy.aspx.**

References

Briggs, M. and Hansen, A. (in press) *Play-based learning in the primary school.* London: Sage.

Coughlin, P.K. (2010) Making field trips count: Collaborating for meaningful experiences. *Social Studies*, 101: 200–210.

Copping, A. (2011) Curriculum approaches, in A. Hansen (ed.) *Primary professional studies.* Exeter: Learning Matters: 23–43.

Dannels, D.P. and Housley-Gaffney, A.L. (2009) Communication across the curriculum and in the disciplines: A call for scholarly cross-curricular advocacy. *Communication Education*, 58 (1): 124–153.

DfEE (1998) *Health and safety of pupils on educational visits.* Available at **http://media.education.gov.uk/assets/files/pdf/h/hspv2.pdf** (accessed 20/3/11).

Haigh, J. (2009) Uses and limitations of mathematics in sport. *Institute of Mathematics and its Applications Journal of Management Mathematics,* 20: 97–108.

Liu, X.S. (2007) The effect of teacher influence at school on first-year teacher attrition: A multilevel analysis of the schools and staffing survey for 1999–2000. *Educational Research and Evaluation*, 13 (1): 1–16.

Meijer, J. (2007) Cross-curricular skills testing in the Netherlands. *The Curriculum Journal*, 18 (2): 155–173.

Noel, A.M. (2007) Elements of a winning field trip. *Kappa Delta Pi Record*, 44 (1): 42–44.

QCDA (2002) *Designing and timetabling the primary curriculum.* QCA/02/912. London: QCDA.

Trudeau, F. and Shephard, R.J. (2008) Physical education, school physical activity, school sports and academic performance. *International Journal of Behavioral Nutrition and Physical Activity*, 5: 1–12.

Wedell, K., Stevens, C. and Waller, T. (2008) Music lessons and inclusion. *British Journal of Special Education*, 35 (3): 181.

7. Using assessment data to improve learning and teaching

Learning Outcomes
....

This chapter explores:
- the need to learn about data;
- the necessity for data collection;
- the processes involved in data collection;
- how data are used;
- targets and target setting;
- setting;
- reporting to parents and carers.

Professional Standards for QTS

Q1 Have high expectations of children and young people including a commitment to ensuring that they can achieve their full educational potential and to establishing fair, respectful, trusting, supportive and constructive relationships with them.

Q3 (a) Be aware of the professional duties of teachers and the statutory framework within which they work.

Q4 Communicate effectively with children, young people, colleagues, parents and carers.

Q7 (b) Identify priorities for their early professional development in the context of induction.

Q8 Have a creative and constructively critical approach towards innovation, being prepared to adapt their practice where benefits and improvements are identified.

Q11 Know the assessment requirements and arrangements for the subjects/ curriculum areas they are trained to teach, including those relating to public examinations and qualifications.

Q12 Know a range of approaches to assessment, including the importance of formative assessment.

Q13 Know how to use local and national statistical information to evaluate the effectiveness of their teaching, to monitor the progress of those they teach and to raise levels of attainment.

Q19 Know how to make effective personalised provision for those they teach, including those for whom English is an additional language or who have special educational needs or disabilities, and how to take practical account of diversity and promote equality and inclusion in their teaching.

Q26 (a) Make effective use of a range of assessment, monitoring and recording strategies.
(b) Assess the learning needs of those they teach in order to set challenging learning objectives.
Q27 Provide timely, accurate and constructive feedback on learners' attainment, progress and areas for development.
Q28 Support and guide learners to reflect on their learning, identify the progress they have made and identify their emerging learning needs.
Q29 Evaluate the impact of their teaching on the progress of all learners, and modify their planning and classroom practice where necessary.

Introduction

In Chapters 2–5 we showed you how mathematics can be used and learned within other subjects. However, the level of achievement by each child in mathematics will still need to be recorded and used to ensure that the most appropriate work is set. This chapter will discuss the need to collect data both in the classroom and across the whole school. We will offer a critical explanation as to why you need to do this, what happens to these data and how they are used to classify schools to parents and the government.

Although there are policy documents produced by local authorities that are standard across all schools, every school will interpret these to suit their own particular needs. In just the same way it is important that you adapt your practice to suit both your own style of recording and the expectations of the particular school that you are working in.

For assessment to be effective it needs to be focused (Mince and Ebersole, 2008). Opportunities to observe and record children's achievements should be included in the planning process rather than assessment being something that is 'done to' children.

Throughout your training and particularly on placement in school you will have been expected to reflect on your own knowledge and understanding of the requirements of the teaching profession regarding assessment. You may well have been asked to provide evidence of how you have assessed children and what you intend to do with the assessment data once collected.

This chapter will outline some of the assessment data collection that occurs within school and how this links to your placement experience. Assessment data are not the only source of evidence you have access to for improving learning and teaching. Indeed, later in this chapter we question the extent to which some data are helping or hindering improvement. However, carrying out a small-scale research project in school could form part of your study and if this is the case you will be expected to collect data to analyse and discuss. Chapter 8 examines more closely how you will use data to inform your assignments.

This chapter begins by detailing some of the reasons why you need to understand and use data. The types of data that you may collect as a trainee teacher and later as a teacher are discussed, before considering how these data are used. We then move on to show how these data are used locally and nationally to provide a picture of schools. To finish we explain how targets are set and levels of children's attainment are reported to parents and carers.

Why do I need to learn about using assessment data?

In all aspects of our lives, data are used to evaluate and improve what we do. For example, all businesses are legally required to log accidents and near-accidents and demonstrate what has been done in response to avoid the likelihood of the accident reoccurring. Many organisations give their employees targets to achieve, using these as a type of incentive to improve productivity or quality. Others use targets to keep things on track. In relation to teacher training, the Training and Development Agency for Schools (TDA) provides targets to every training provider for the number of trainee teachers they should recruit every year (**www.tda.gov.uk/training-provider/itt/funding-allocations.aspx**). This target setting ensures that market forces (in this case the number of teachers required to fill positions throughout the country) are met. The remainder of this section continues to focus on how data are used in education.

How data are used to improve your own education

While studying at school and throughout your time in higher education a great deal of data will have been collected about you. This will have been fed into spreadsheets and databases to produce statistics that evaluate the impact of the pedagogy of your ITT provider. Universities and employment-based routes into teaching are judged externally and internally from data produced by the National Student Survey and Newly Qualified Teacher Survey data. Institutions use the data to identify issues that have been raised. Recommendations are made from this for validation of modules and the results they produce are used for reflection and improvement of courses in the future.

In all aspects of your ITT programme – including while on placement and during seminars or assessments – your own subject knowledge of mathematics is monitored. As a result some form of assessment and feedback will be given to you to enable you to address any gaps. This may take the form of subject audits and grids setting out the QTS Standards to enable you to identify progression from 'satisfactory' to 'good' and 'outstanding'. As a trainee professional you will be expected to reflect on your own learning. Through discussion with tutors and school-based mentors, you will also be expected to be able to show how you are addressing these needs. Setting yourself effective and relevant targets linked to the QTS standards will inform your progression through your NQT year.

A national perspective: Curriculum development

The government and Ofsted use school data to inform changes to the curriculum and the emphasis that will be placed on particular subject areas. Literacy and mathematics were a major focus in the 1990s, resulting in the introduction of the National Literacy and Numeracy Strategies followed by the Primary National Strategy and then the National Strategies. With the publication of the Williams Report (DfES, 2008), mathematics pedagogy and subject content continue to be high on the government's agenda. Analysis of available data is crucial in order for clear goals to be set and effective change to take place. Chapter 8 explores this in more detail.

Why do I need to collect assessment data?

Data can be used to inform teachers' policy and pedagogy. You will have benefited yourself from your own teachers' and lecturers' use of your assessment grades, module evaluations and so on. As a trainee teacher, you have a key role to play in supporting your placement schools to use data effectively to support children's learning within mathematics and across the curriculum.

Assessment for learning

Assessing children's attainment in mathematics is carried out in several ways throughout the school year, from the individual child through to the whole school. In order for children to progress and for you to teach at the most appropriate level, data from any assessment need to be considered throughout your planning. This type of assessment is known as assessment for learning (AfL) and is formative and ongoing.

Research Focus: Inside the black box

In 1998 Paul Black and Dylan Wiliam published *Inside the black box: Raising standards through classroom assessment*. Why inside the 'black box'? Black and Wiliam (1998, page 1) explain:

> In terms of systems engineering, present [education] policy seems to treat the classroom as a black box. Certain inputs from the outside are fed in or make demands – pupils, teachers, other resources, management rules and requirements, parental anxieties, tests with pressures to score highly, and so on. Some outputs follow, hopefully pupils who are more knowledgeable and competent, better test results, teachers who are more or less satisfied, and more or less exhausted. But what is happening inside?

This booklet paved the way for the significant wave of assessment for learning that was introduced into primary schools soon after. In order to make sense of the plethora of advice and guidance that followed, we return to the principles that Black and Wiliam (pages 9–13) introduced in this seminal publication.

→

The self-esteem of pupils

Feedback to any pupil should be about the particular qualities of his of her work, with advice on what he or she can do to improve, and should avoid comparisons with other pupils.

Self-assessment for pupils

For formative assessment to be productive, pupils should be trained in self-assessment so that they can understand the main purposes of their learning and thereby grasp what they need to do to achieve.

The evolution of effective teaching

Opportunities for pupils to express their understanding should be designed into any piece of teaching, for this will initiate the interaction whereby formative assessment aids learning.

The dialogue between pupils and a teacher should be thoughtful, reflective, focused to evoke and explore understanding, and conducted so that all pupils have an opportunity to think and to express their ideas.

Tests and homework exercises can be an invaluable guide to learning, but the exercises must be clear and relevant to learning aims. The feedback on them should give each pupil guidance on how to improve, and each must be given opportunity and help to work at the improvement.

Activity

Reflect on the assessment for learning tasks or opportunities that you have carried out or observed on placements. To what extent were they reflecting the founding principles identified above?

To what extent were the children really in control of the assessment, compared to your or their teacher's control? If you were carrying out the assessments, did you understand the purpose of what you were doing?

While on placement you will normally be expected to include your assessment criteria on your lesson plans and then record your knowledge of the children's attainment. This recording will be used by your class teacher and the school after you have finished your placement, as well as for your own planning during your placement.

Assessment of learning

Data inform the overall picture of achievement across the school ready to become part of the school improvement plan (SIP) and hence provide the school management team (SMT) with evidence to set targets and ensure that the most appropriate level of support is in place for mathematics for the following year. Any form of assessment or data collection should help you to reflect on the effectiveness of your pedagogical approach both at classroom level and at school level.

Collecting data

The standards for QTS require you to know the requirements for assessment in primary schools (Q11) as well as be able to carry out assessment (Q26, 27, 28). Throughout this section and the next, 'What happens to the assessment data?', both these elements are addressed.

Collecting formative assessment data

There is little point in producing a placement file that is bulging with a wealth of charts with various coding for every child in the class, but which is mostly meaningless in terms of actual hard evidence that can be used to inform and improve learning and pedagogy. As you read the case study below think about your own experiences on placement and whether Farhat's experience reflects your own.

Case Study: Recording children's achievement

Farhat is a trainee nearing the midpoint of her second placement in a Year 2 class. Although she is able to talk about the achievement of the children, she has produced no written evidence of recording the children's achievement. She has agreed the target of compiling evidence to bring to her weekly meeting with her mentor.

Below is the sheet that Farhat shared with her mentor, Mary, and the discussion that followed.

Name	Observe, handle and describe common 2D and 3D shapes;name and describe the mathematical features of common 2D and 3D shapes, including triangles of various kinds, rectangles including squares, circles, cubes, cuboids, then hexagons, pentagons, cylinders, pyramids, cones and spheres
Amy	✗
Beatrice	✓✓
Cameron	✓✓
Dulcie	✓
Ellen	✓✓
Farzana	✓
George	✓✓
Hetty	✓✓

→

Ibrahim	✓✓
Josephine	✓✓
Kathryn	✓
Liam	✓
Marina	✗
Nathan	✗
Omar	✓✓
Penelope	✓✓
Quentin	✓✓
Rosie	✓✓
Sanchez	✓✓
Tanya	✓✓
Ursula	✓✓
Victoria	✓
Wesley	✓
Xavier	✓✓
Yvette	✓✓
Zafina	✓✓
Zak	✓✓

Figure 7.1 Farhat's recording of the children's achievement

M: I am really pleased that you have taken this target so seriously and produced such a thorough document, Farhat. However, before I make any comment I would like you to talk me through what you have done, please.

F: Well as we discussed in our last meeting, I needed to be able to show you evidence that I am assessing during the lesson so I made a class list and as I was working with groups and individuals I marked off who had got it and who had not.

M: Can you explain what the symbols mean please and at what level you think these children are working?

F: Right, ok. Two ticks means they have got it, one tick means they have nearly got it and a cross means they haven't got it at all. To be honest I'm not exactly sure what level this is as I was using the teacher's plans, but I think that Year 2 children should be working at level 2.

M: Ok. What was the focus of the session? You seem to have several learning outcomes together so it is quite difficult when you say that the child has achieved something to know what exactly this is.

F: Ah yes, I see what you mean.

M: You have also not indicated which class this is and when this assessment took place. This is needed if we are going to make use of this information once you have left.

F: Of course yes. When you point these things out it seems so obvious that I can't believe I didn't think of it. I will add those things and prepare another sheet ready for our meeting next week.

M: That would be really good and during the week you might want to speak to the other staff about how they record their assessment and collect some ideas that you could use on your next placements.

F: Thanks, that would be great.

Mary is pleased that Farhat is able to provide a clearer picture of attainment than previously. Mary explains the need for her to be more aware of the level at which the children are working and together they set this as Farhat's next target.

Links to the National Curriculum

In the case study above, Farhat provided assessment data from a lesson she had taught on shape. (Ma3 2b Observe, handle and describe common 2D and 3D shapes; name and describe the mathematical features of common 2D and 3D shapes, including triangles of various kinds, rectangles including squares, circles, cubes, cuboids, then hexagons, pentagons, cylinders, pyramids, cones and spheres). Unfortunately by including so much information in the objective it is, as Mary points out, unclear as to what exactly the children have achieved.

Activity

Scrutinise one or two assessment sheets you have used on placement and answer the following questions (inspired by Mince and Ebersole, 2008).

1. How is the assessment purposeful and systematic?
2. How is the assessment helping your lessons to be creative?
3. Is your formative assessment 'risk free' in that it provides feedback to children to enable them to improve their learning without appearing judgemental?
4. How was the assessment used to plan your next lessons?
5. In what ways has the assessment been used to inform others?

If you have already used Assessing Pupil Progress (APP) grids for assessment on placement, revisit these and answer the questions above again. If you have not, download the mathematics APP assessment grid from: **http://nationalstrategies. standards.dcsf.gov.uk/node/47548**. Revisit the questions above and consider how you could use APP grids to address the issues these questions raise. For guidance on APP, see the Further Reading section.

In school you will need to monitor the progress of the children you are teaching. Assessing Pupil Progress (APP) is one form of in-school assessment that helps to track pupils and diagnose strengths and weaknesses that need to be addressed at both individual and group level. As Gurjit discovered in the Chapter 1 case study 'Using assessment evidence from beyond the mathematics lesson', it is difficult as a trainee teacher to have a clear picture of the expectations of each level of attainment and only through discussion with his mentor did Gurjit begin to understand and grasp what these expectations were. Like all other assessment, APP is not an exact science and is based on professional judgement and knowledge of the child over a period of time. There are occasions though when this longer period of time and the ability to reflect on your judgements about a child's attainment and ability are not available. You will simply be presented with raw data and be expected to form opinions taken from them.

If you are on placement in a small school the class could consist of an entire key stage. This presents you with the challenge of assessing and collecting data across many different levels. As a classroom teacher you will need to be aware of and be familiar with not only the level of attainment of the children in your class but also the expected levels of attainment below and above in order to plan accordingly and offer the most appropriate level of learning opportunities for your class. This in turn will inform how to move the children on in order to ensure that they progress and have covered the essential content from the curriculum. As a result you will be ensuring that children are as prepared as they can be to undertake the more formal SATs at the end of Year 6.

Summative data

As a trainee teacher one of the most important pieces of information you will need to know before you can begin to plan is the attainment level of the children. This can be gained from both teacher assessment and formal assessments such as SAT tests. Additionally, once you qualify and take up a new position you will probably be given information about the children you will be teaching. Among this may well be copies of their Early Years Foundation Stage Profile, Year 2 SAT results, National Curriculum levels from teacher assessment or from practice SATs papers from the previous year. This will very often be given to you before you even meet the children and you will need to begin to form a picture of the ability levels ready to inform your planning for the start of the year.

Levelling children's work

For many trainee teachers and teachers, assessing and levelling children's work is something they can initially find quite difficult (Hall and Harding, 2002). With so much content in the curriculum they can feel at a loss as to what should be assessed and what should not. Even when the focus for assessment has been established, how to record achievement in the most effective and useful way needs to be decided upon. As previously mentioned, no trainee wants to be overwhelmed with meaningless paperwork any more than a school wishes to have copious amounts of unnecessary assessment data. In the earlier case study, 'Recording children's achievement', Farhat commented that she thought that Year 2 children should be working at level 2. Working at or within National Curriculum level 2 is the expectation of a child of this age. However, in any one class there could be a wide range of ability levels. To address this, some schools 'set' children in attainment groups. If this is the case, there is a need to have clear recording methods across the school and staff will need to liaise about each child's progress. You can read more about setting later in this chapter.

What are 'standards'?

The Cambridge Review (Alexander, 2010 pages 328–9) makes a distinction between two definitions of the word 'standards'.

1. *Standards as 'what is attained'*: the identification of the standard is made by a judgement on actual performance or behaviour.

2. *Standards as 'what to aim for'*: the level of performance or behaviour that is considered to be desirable.

In order to make this most pertinent to you, we ask you to carry out the activity that follows in relation to the standards that you are required to demonstrate in order to achieve QTS.

Activity

Reflect on your understanding of the standards for QTS. Can you see them both as something to aim for as well as something to attain? How does your ITT provider support you in seeing the standards as both of these things?

Now imagine this. You are coming toward the end of your ITT programme. You have undertaken a rich, varied and interesting course up to this point. However, your provider has changed the way that you will be assessed on the standards for QTS. Next week you will be required to sit a small number of 45-minute tests that will assess your level of attainment in each of the QTS standards. The results of these will be published in your end-of-course reference to prospective employers and the results will also be used by the TDA to allocate further numbers of new trainee teachers to your provider in the future.

How did the second part of the activity make you feel?

Did you perceive any levels of anxiety? Pulwain (2008, page 1026) identifies that *what is certain is that the results of tests and examinations can form the basis of young people's self-judgements, aspirations and fears. For a small proportion ... they become a serious obstacle to demonstrating academic achievement and also relate to myriad difficulties in other areas of life...* Did you wonder what future employers might think of you if you did not achieve the grades you'd hoped for in the tests? Perhaps you were concerned about the impact of your grades on the future of your ITT provider.

Did you feel that the method of assessment was 'unfair'? If you felt that it was unfair, you may have been thinking about all the other evidence you have gathered from your course that demonstrates your achievements in relation to the standards. This 'unfairness' can also be seen in children's SATs: *However, it should not be forgotten ... that this information is about attainment in* tests, *which is not necessarily the same as attainment in the national curriculum* (Alexander, 2010 page 331). The case study below illustrates this.

Case study: Interpretation of SAT scores

Martin is a trainee teacher on his final block placement. SAT results have been received by the school and children have been given their individual results. The class teacher tells the class that the Year 7 cohort leader from the secondary school will be visiting to assign them to groups for next year based on their SAT scores.

Martin observes one child, Andrew, becoming quite distressed as he receives his results and realises that he will be in the lower attainment groups for everything. All year he has been one of the more able mathematicians and has always been able to discuss science experiments and results. In fact he has created a working lighthouse in design and technology and been able to begin to develop his own strategies for finding the nth term of a series. He has always struggled with English comprehension so was not surprised that he received a level 3 for this. It was the level 3 for mathematics and science that was the surprise as he had been predicted a level 4 or above for both subjects.

This case study gives an example of the care needed when interpreting summative assessment results. The main problem in this case would appear to have been Andrew's comprehension of the questions. He was able to read the words but not assimilate these in a way that enabled him to make sense of the text to complete the questions. For children who struggle to read (that is, decode the text) there is provision within the delivery of the mathematics and science SATs to have a reader. However, there is no provision to help children's comprehension skills. On close analysis of the papers it was clear that Andrew was more than able to complete numeric calculation questions but struggled with word problems. This would suggest that a child's inability to comprehend has an impact on their ability to access much of the curriculum.

SATs results are published annually, making this information available to a wider audience including Ofsted and parents of both existing and prospective pupils. This 'high stakes' testing impacts on schools' curriculum planning and teachers' pedagogy, as the research focus below shows.

....

Research Focus: The impact of SATs

The Cambridge Review (Alexander, 2010) provides an authoritative overview of the research that has been carried out about the impact National Curriculum assessment has on children and teachers. The report identifies research that has shown how many schools 'teach to the test', narrowing their curriculum in the process. The report challenges the reality of this perception by noting research that suggests that *exciting and creative lessons do more to advance basic skills than any narrow focus on them* (pages 331-2) but also identifies that there is a tension between what the government says schools should be doing (in terms of a broad and balanced curriculum) and perceived priorities through target setting and testing.

Furthermore, there is evidence that schools focus on 'borderline' children, where teachers focus more on the children who, with additional support, are likely to achieve level 4 in the tests. This may explain why there is a significant gap between lower and higher achievement of children and raises a number of ethical issues that you may wish to consider as a trainee teacher.

....

What happens to the assessment data?

How the government uses data

The government uses data to evidence their evaluations about the impact of curriculum policy and guidance. However, the Cambridge Review (Alexander, 2010) raises a question about the extent to which the SATs results demonstrate a true reflection of a raise of attainment through questioning the validity of the tests being comparable each year.

The review warns that it is difficult to make a clear judgement on trends about children's attainment over time because different tests are used each year. However, if we do look at SATs results from 1995 to 2008 at face value to identify a trend, broadly speaking in English, mathematics and science children's attainment in Key Stage 1 and Key Stage 2 steeply rose until 2000, and after that period there has been around a 1 per cent rise in attainment each year. In 2008 this resulted in 81 per cent of children achieving level 4 in English, 78 per cent in mathematics and 85 per cent in science.

It is important for you to be aware that when SATs were first developed, level 4 was the expected level of attainment for an average child. Therefore, recent target setting shows that there is now a very high expectation on most children to achieve what was previously set as an average.

How schools use data

The previous section heightened our awareness of some of the pitfalls of taking national testing data at face value. However, SATs results produce the data set that is used by schools and so this section looks at how these data, once they have been collected, are used to make judgements about school performance.

Although schools collect their own formative assessment data for use within the school, much of the summative assessment data are collected and published in the form of pupil performance data. This information has been stored in many forms over the years and is presently managed through RAISEonline which *provides interactive analysis of school and pupil performance data. It replaces the Ofsted Performance and Assessment (PANDA) reports and DCSF's Pupil Achievement Tracker (PAT)* (Ofsted and DfE, online).

RAISEonline aims to:

- *Enable schools to analyse performance data in greater depth as part of the self-evaluation process,*

- *Provide a common set of analyses for schools, Local authorities, inspectors and School Improvement Partners,*

- *Better support teaching and learning.*

Features include:

- *Reports and analysis covering the attainment and progress of pupils in Key Stage 1, 2, 3 & 4, with interactive features allowing exploration of hypotheses about pupil performance.*

- *Contextual information about the school including comparisons to schools nationally,*

- *Question level analysis, allowing schools to investigate the performance of pupils in specific curriculum areas,*

- *Target Setting, supporting schools in the process of monitoring, challenging and supporting pupil performance,*

- *Data management facility providing the ability to import and edit pupil level data and create school-defined fields and teaching groups.*

(Ofsted and DfE, online)

The extract above shows how schools are expected to analyse their data and apply the findings to inform school improvement. The next activity asks you to analyse some authentic school data yourself.

Activity

Here is a snapshot of the type of information you may be given about a particular school.

Background Information

Total number of pupils on roll (all ages)	**300**
Pupils with statements of SEN or supported at School Action Plus: number	**50**
Pupils with statements of SEN or supported at School Action Plus: percentage	**17%**
Pupils with SEN, supported at School Action: number	**60**
Pupils with SEN, supported at School Action: percentage	**20%**
Number of pupils on roll aged 10 as at 31 August (Previous year)	**40**

Key Stage 2 Test Results

Published eligible pupil number	**40**
Eligible pupils with SEN with a statement or supported at School Action Plus: number	**2**
Eligible pupils with SEN with a statement or supported at School Action Plus: percentage	**5%**
Eligible pupils with SEN supported at School Action: number	**10**
Eligible pupils with SEN supported at School Action: percentage	**25%**

English

Percentage of pupils achieving level 4 or above in English	**80%**
Percentage of children achieving level 5 in English	**50%**
Percentage of pupils absent from or not able to access the tests in English	**0%**

Mathematics

Percentage of pupils achieving level 4 or above in mathematics	**100%**
Percentage of pupils achieving level 5 in mathematics	**50%**
Percentage of pupils absent from or not able to access the tests in mathematics	**0%**

Science

Percentage of pupils achieving level 4 or above in science	**100%**
Percentage of pupils achieving level 5 in science	**70%**
Percentage of pupils absent from or not able to access the tests in science	**0%**

Try to answer the following questions using the above information.

What is your initial impression of the level of attainment of the school?
In which subject do children seem to be underperforming?
Which subject has the best results?
How many children achieved level 5 in English?

Targets and target setting

One significant aspect of the teacher's role is being able to effectively gather, represent, interpret and use data in a variety of ways and with a variety of different people. One such person will be the mathematics subject leader in the school who has the responsibility of monitoring the standard of mathematics learning across the whole school. The subject leader will report to the senior management team (SMT) and to staff at regular intervals. Clear school targets in line with performance expectations linked to national statistics can then be set.

In a similar way in the classroom, children need to be involved in any targets set for them that are used on a daily basis. School targets for attainment are set by the government and schools are expected to strive to achieve these. Much time is spent by the SMT of schools analysing data and prioritising resources to maintain and continue to try to improve performance with an aim of meeting these government targets. Each year after SAT tests have been completed the results are published in *Achievement and attainment tables* (**www.education.gov.uk/ performancetables/**).

Setting

In some schools it may be decided that setting by ability is the most effective way to improve performance. This will involve a good deal of decision-making regarding which children are put into which group. Many factors have to be considered alongside the actual raw data. In many schools children work in ability groups for English and mathematics. Sometimes due to the constraints of the timetable, children will be in the same attainment group for both subjects as this is the only way the timetable will work.

Activity

The secondary school Year 7 cohort leader needs to sort out the groups for children moving in the new school year.

Using the information below from a Year 6 cohort sort the children into mathematics groups and English groups.

Name	English	Maths
Amy	5	5
Beatrice	3	3
Cameron	3	3
Dulcie	2	3
Ellen	4	4
Farzana	4	4
George	5	5
Hetty	4	4
Ibrahim	4	4
Josephine	4	3

Kathryn	2	2
Liam	4	3
Marina	4	4
Nathan	4	4
Omar	4	4
Penelope	5	5
Quentin	4	4
Rosie	3	4
Sanchez	4	5
Tanya	4	4
Ursula	4	5
Victoria	4	5
Wesley	4	5
Xavier	3	3
Yvette	5	5
Zafina	5	5
Zak	5	5

Now try to answer the following questions for each grouping system.

How did you sort the groups?
Do you think this is the most effective division?
How would you justify the sizes of the groups to parents?
How long would you keep children in these groups?
What would be your criteria for children moving groups?

The school has now informed you that, due to timetabling constraints, the children will be taught in the same group for mathematics and English. Would you rearrange the groups at all? What criteria would you use?

You may already have firm views on the advantages and disadvantages of setting within school. Did the activity change your mind? You may want to reflect on why children are often grouped according to their English attainment for other curriculum subjects, such as science. What are the implications of this for the children? When you are next on placement you might want to discuss the school's rationale for setting or not setting. You might also like to consider how you would inform parents once you have grouped or not grouped children.

How parents use data

Deciding on the most appropriate school to send their child to is an important decision for many parents. After all, how do they know the difference between one school and the next? For some it is through the location or a recommendation of friends and family, for others the fact that siblings are already attending the school. However, many make the decision based on data about the school. Most schools will have a school profile or handbook which they give out to prospective parents. School websites are becoming more professional and informative. School Ofsted reports are available on the internet, as are the tables published each year after SATs have been marked.

Achievement and attainment tables

The Primary School Performance Tables give more than one measure of a school's performance. These measures can be considered alongside each other when evaluating the performance of a school. The Tables show:

–   *background information for each school, including the number and percentage of pupils in the school (a) with statements of Special Educational Needs (SEN) or with SEN supported at School Action Plus; and (b) with SEN supported at School Action*

–   *a Contextual Value Added (CVA) measure and coverage percentage*

–   *the number of pupils eligible for KS2 assessment including the number and percentage of KS2 pupils (a) with statements of SEN or with SEN supported at School Action Plus; and (b) with SEN supported at School Action*

–   *the percentage of pupils achieving Level 4 and above and Level 5 at KS2, and the percentage of pupils absent from or unable to access the tests*

–   *the percentage of pupils making at least expected progress in English, and separately, in maths, between the end of KS1 and end of KS2*

–   *bar charts showing the average point score in English and maths for the past four years*

–   *bar charts showing comparative results in % level 4+ in both English & maths for the past three years*

–   *the percentages of overall, unauthorised and persistent absence.*

(www.education.gov.uk/performancetables/primary_10/p2.shtml)

It is possible for a school to be overachieving in the context of the school but underachieving when compared to national data. Think back to Andrew in the earlier case study 'Interpretation of SATs' and his achievement. For this reason it is important that other factors are taken into account when judging school performance. Perhaps a more realistic picture of a school is achieved when taking into account things other than raw data. Value-added data might be a better measurement of children's progression. In order to gain a feel for the schools that are the most appropriate for their children, prospective parents often take tours before making decisions.

Communicating with parents and carers

Much time is spent by schools and the government developing a curriculum that is fit for purpose. We mentioned above how mathematics curriculum guidance has changed several times over the last decade. In fact it is still changing, with the DfE's curriculum review under way (see Further Reading for more on the curriculum review). This case study shows how one mathematics co-ordinator helped parents to understand the curriculum changes at her school.

Case Study: Introducing curriculum change to parents

With constant change comes the need for clear understanding by all concerned. The introduction of the National Numeracy Strategy (1999) and the changes to calculation methods was at the time seen by some people, both parents/carers and teachers, as unnecessary. In one typical school, many parents asked questions such as:

What was wrong with the way we were taught? It hasn't done us any harm!

Why do children need to understand as long as they can do it?

What's wrong with learning the tables by rote – didn't hurt me!

When is Julie going to be doing 'proper' sums?

Why isn't there anything written in Charlie's book?'

As you can imagine, for the mathematics co-ordinator, Sue, introducing these new ideas was quite a daunting experience. She had to convince reluctant staff to embrace new ideas and also provide support to parents/carers. To support parents, Sue:

- designed and sent out leaflets of information explaining all the new calculation methods and ways in which parents/carers could work with their children;

- led adult classes to explain and give opportunities for them to experience working with the new ideas;

- arranged for parent/carer's evenings to discuss worries.

Gradually as these new methods of calculating became embedded into the school's curriculum the need for this extra support began to decline. Parents, staff and children became more familiar with new ideas and discovered that some were actually helping to improve learning. Now booklets and further guidance are on the school website for parents to access.

It is possible to see a booklet that one school provides to parents at **www.milkingbank.com/cms/media/lettershome/CalculationPolicy-Year4-6-ABookletforParents.pdf**

Throughout this book we have tried to show how mathematics by its very nature forms part of many other subjects, how learning and understanding can be enhanced by combining different curriculum subjects. In order for this approach to be successful, the need to involve parents in the process once again becomes necessary.

Learning Outcomes Review

This chapter has outlined the need for you to collect appropriate data for use within school and to inform a wider audience including parents and the government. The many processes that this data goes through have been discussed and the importance of communicating with parents and carers has been highlighted.

Self-assessment questions

1. Use a diagram to show the relationship between the following stakeholders, to map the reporting processes in school: head teacher, school management team, parent, governors, child, teacher, school improvement partner (SIP) from the local authority, Department for Education.
2. Name as many different types of assessment as you can.
3. Identify similarities between the use of APP to assess children's learning and the way in which you are assessed against the standards for QTS.

Further Reading

To read more about assessment for learning, you may be interested in reading further from the Black Box series. These include:

- Assessment Reform Group (1999) *Assessment for learning: Beyond the black box.* Cambridge: University of Cambridge.

- Black, P., Harrison, C., Lee, C., Marshall, B. and Wiliam, D. (2002) *Working inside the black box: Assessment for learning in the classroom.* London: nferNelson Publishing Company Ltd.

- Hodgen, J. and Wiliam, D. (2006) *Mathematics inside the black box: Assessment for learning in the mathematics classroom.* nferNelson Publishing Company Ltd.

Briggs, M. (2011) Assessment, in Hansen, A. (ed.) *Primary professional studies.* Exeter: Learning Matters. This provides a detailed explanation of the legal requirements for reporting to parents.

DfE *Curriculum Review* information can be found at **www.education.gov.uk/schools/ teachingandlearning/curriculum/nationalcurriculum**

Eady, S. (2011) Personal professional development, in Hansen, A. (ed.) *Primary Professional Studies.* Exeter: Learning Matters. This discusses performance management and how this is developed from your ITT programme and throughout your career.

National Strategies *Assessing pupil progress* (online) provides guidance on assessing pupil progress (APP). Visit **http://nationalstrategies.standards.dcsf.gov.uk/node/20683**

References

Alexander, R. (ed.) (2010) *Children, their world, their education: Final report and recommendations of the Cambridge Primary Review.* London: Routledge.

Black, P and Wiliam, D. (1998) *Inside the black box: Raising standards through classroom assessment.* London: nferNelson Publishing Company Ltd.

Briggs, M. (2011) Assessment, in Hansen, A. (ed.) *Primary professional studies.* Exeter: Learning Matters: 184–203.

Hall, K. and Harding, A. (2002) Level descriptions and teacher assessment in England: towards a community of assessment practice. *Educational Research*, 44 (1): 1–15.

Mince, R. and Ebersole, T. (2008) An effective assessment model for implementing change and improving learning. *Community College Journal of Research and Practice,* 32: 871–876.

Ofsted and Department for Education (online) *About Raiseonline* Available at **https://www.raiseonline.org/About.aspx** (accessed 21/3/11).

Pulwain, D. (2008) Examination stress and text anxiety. *Psychologist*, 21 (12): 1026–1029.

8. Developing teaching and learning through research

Introduction

This chapter introduces what we refer to as the improving teaching and learning process. This process is one that you can use in all your assessed coursework during your initial teacher training course, not just your mathematics education assignments. We present it to you here because there is much mathematical knowledge, skill and understanding that you require in order to undertake the process. However, the literature review section does use mathematics-based literature in order to explore how cross-curricular teaching is currently being addressed.

This case study illustrates how the improving teaching and learning process you carry out during your module assessments can be used as a tool for your professional development. After the case study we will introduce you to the process by providing an overview of each of the elements. Following that, each element will be further developed including case studies, activities and literature to support your understanding.

Case Study: Using educational research to develop teaching and learning

Ben was a PGCE trainee teacher who was studying on a Masters' level research module called, 'Improving teaching and learning through research' halfway through his course. Having come to the course with a 2:1 Honours degree in the sciences, he was struggling to understand the social science methodologies that he was expected to select from.

Instead, he wanted to form a control group in his class, undertake an intervention with half of them and analyse pre- and post-test results in a quantitative way. His tutor pointed out to him that because his class had 30 children in it, having 'control' and 'intervention' groups of 15 was not statistically viable and so she encouraged him instead, to think about more qualitative ways that he could still explore the issue that interested him.

Unconvinced, he went on his five-week placement, carried out the case study research and submitted an assignment. Both Ben and his tutor were disappointed at the quality of the assignment, and Ben did not achieve a mark at Masters' standard. Ben commented to his tutor that he really didn't understand the whole point of educational research, that it was 'soft' and that he hadn't learned anything from it.

Given the timescale of his PGCE, it was only after his final placement that Ben and his tutor could meet formally so Ben could be supported to resubmit his assignment. Ben's tutor recalls:

> I'd booked a computer room for tutorials and had invited those students who needed to rework their assignments to come along. Ben came with his assignment on a memory stick, sat at a computer and began typing. I wanted to target Ben early in the tutorial as he had been so despondent during the module and I was frustrated with myself that I hadn't convinced him of the value of research as a tool to develop his teaching.

> When I went to sit next to him he said, 'I'm alright now, you know.' I asked him what he meant and he said that he had 'got it'. He said that he met new children in his final placement classroom who were exhibiting the same difficulties with the mathematics topic he had chosen to focus on for his research. He said that it all fell into place as the reading he had completed and the analysis of the case study evidence he'd collected a few months earlier all came flooding back. He told me that it resonated with his new context and although he'd been originally frustrated that he couldn't generalise from his findings, he could see how his teaching had developed because of the very focused way that he had investigated the mathematical thinking of one particular child in his case study.

$\rightarrow$

When Ben resubmitted his assignment it was awarded a grade of 75 per cent. The transformation was remarkable. It was only at his graduation some months later that I was able to catch up with him again. He explained that during the block placement he had realised the value of educational research as a tool for professional development. He also said that he was able to talk about his research and how it had impacted on his final placement during a job interview, and that later he'd found out that his ability to talk about being a practitioner researcher was what made him stand out from the other candidates.

The case study shows how one trainee teacher began to understand the value of using the improving teaching and learning process as a means of professional development. It also shows how it provided him with the tools to be able critically to analyse children's learning in a new setting and he was able to communicate his own learning about that with his prospective employers.

The improving teaching and learning process

All your ITT assignments are designed to develop your teaching and therefore the children's learning throughout your course. If you keep this in mind, you will see the process as a whole and this will help you to see it as a valuable part of your training rather than a series of disjointed hoops that you are required to jump through.

Figure 8.1 shows a diagrammatic representation of the improving teaching and learning process – our interpretation of how you will normally carry out your assignments – and this also presents an outline of the structure of the remainder of this chapter.

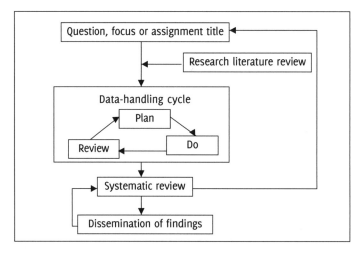

Figure 8.1 The improving teaching and learning process

An overview of the teaching and learning process

Here we present an overview of the teaching and learning process in Figure 8.1 so you can broadly understand how the process works. More detail about each element follows this overview.

Beginnings

By setting or being set a question, area of focus, or the title of an assignment, you start the process of improving your teaching and the children's learning. This start presents you with the problem that you will be exploring.

Literature review

Reading research literature that explores issues around the area you are focusing on will help you to develop your ideas. First, you will broaden and deepen your understanding through learning more than you know. Second, some of the literature you will read will challenge what you currently think. The mathematical skills involved during the literature review include using Boolean logic to search for appropriate literature, organising your reading, perhaps by using a database to keep tabs on your references, and classifying and organising your notes.

Once you are a substantial part of the way through your literature review, you will be in a position to think about how you want to address the issues and so begin to think about collecting data.

The data-handling cycle

We have crudely referred to this part of the process as the data-handling cycle. You may recall that in Chapter 5 we outlined a three-part cycle that it is possible to see in many aspects of your teaching which we referred to as a 'plan, do, review' cycle. It is also present during the improving teaching and learning process as you will see here.

Plan

It is at this point that you begin to think about what kind of data you will collect, how you will collect them and how you will present them. Crucially you need to ask yourself, 'will these data help inform my question, issue or title?' You will need to think about whether you will collect qualitative or quantitative data, as well as consider the constraints you will be working within. For example, what timescales do you have to commit to data collection? How many participants will be involved?

Do

In a research project, 'doing' might begin with a pilot study, or you may read a paper about someone else's research which you replicate and compare your results. A pilot study generally uses a very small sample to see if your question or method of data collection will enable you to achieve an answer. If you are collecting data to support a smaller assignment, you will begin by identifying which participants you will be involving. In all cases you will need to follow your ITT provider's and the school's ethical guidance for carrying out research and ensure you have all the appropriate permissions.

Review

Once collected, data must be collated and represented in order to make sense of them. The skills required in collating data vary depending on the type of data you have collected. Additionally, you will need to consider how best to collate and represent the data to inform your question, issue or title as effectively as possible.

Systematic review

When you are a trainee, the pace with which you are normally expected to carry out all aspects of your course does not often allow you an opportunity to deeply and meaningfully reflect on how what you are doing can significantly and positively impact on your practice. However, the advantage of engaging in academic work that requires you to make time to bring together your own ideas with those of others (literature) and examples from the classroom or wider school community means you have the opportunity to do this through a systematic review.

When you are systematically reviewing your research, you need to think about (a) what you have discovered, and (b) what you have learned. A systematic review includes considering the validity, reliability and bias of your data.

Dissemination of findings

For many trainees, the assignment that is marked is seen as the main part of the improving teaching and learning process. Although this is the 'product' that is marked, your tutor is actually looking at how you have responded to improving your teaching and the children's learning through the whole process.

Now that the improving teaching and learning process has been summarised, each stage is discussed in detail below, identifying the mathematical skills that you will use.

Beginnings

The teaching and learning process begins with a question, focus or assignment title, intended for you to develop ideas about your teaching to have a positive effect on the children (Lee, 2005). This beginning can be decided on for many reasons. It may simply be that your tutor has given you the title or, if you have some choice over the focus, you pursue a particular interest or follow up a critical incident.

In relation to the mathematical skills you are employing, this beginning becomes a complex problem that you will solve, using enquiry and reasoning. You will be asking yourself questions that begin with 'Why ... ?', 'I wonder if ... ?', 'I'd like to know more about ...', 'How do I respond to ...?'

> **Activity**
>
> Look at a number of assignment titles you have been given. Reflect on how the title and accompanying guidance are intended to help you to improve your teaching.

When you begin, it is most likely that you will have some understanding and opinion on the title, focus or question you have begun with. The literature review helps you to further explore the issues and it is to this that we now turn.

Literature review

Searching research literature

In any assessed work you carry out, you will be expected to use the research literature because:

- it enables you to challenge your own views through what others have learned;
- it demonstrates that you come from a knowledgeable standpoint;
- it justifies the reason for your research or your discussion.

In order to make the most efficient use of your searches, you should employ Boolean logic. This improves the chances of finding research articles that you find useful and so speeds up this element of the process. Organising your reading into a database is another way that you can speed up the process.

Organising your reading and references

By the time you complete your initial teacher training (ITT) you may have read hundreds of reports, articles and books and setting up and maintaining your own record of these data may be a very good use of your time. After all, it is likely that there are references you use in several assignments. If you are starting from scratch every time you find, read and reference these items, you may be wasting time and could benefit from a more streamlined approach.

Electronic databases (such as EndNote, BibTeX, or CiteULike) allow you to search for key words at a later date, avoiding the 'now, where did I read that?' dilemma. It is worth asking your library about the database available through them. It will take a very short time for you to familiarise yourself with how to use it. You are also likely to find that your library's system will allow you to import citations straight to the program. Other search engines are also developing their systems to enable this to happen. Furthermore, these databases create the references list automatically for you, usually in the referencing style that your tutor will expect.

Peer-reviewed and professional journals

How familiar are you with mathematics education journals? There are a number of journals that you can use to read about how children learn mathematics and how teachers can improve their mathematics teaching.

Activity

Visit the library in person or online. Take some time to browse the journals they have, using the list below. Make a note of such things as the aims and purposes of the journal, its intended audiences, any special issues it has recently published, its peer review process, if it is available online and in what country the research was undertaken.

Peer-reviewed journals
Educational Studies in Mathematics
For the Learning of Mathematics
International Journal of Science and Mathematics Education
Journal for Research in Mathematics Education
Journal of Mathematical Behavior
Journal of Mathematics Teacher Education
Mathematical Thinking and Learning
Research in Mathematics Education

Professional journals:
Equals: Mathematics and Special Needs
Mathematics in School
Mathematics Teacher
Mathematics Teaching
Primary Mathematics
Teaching Children Mathematics

This list is designed to get you started. When you are carrying out a literature review you may need to look further afield. Often you will find other journals through the references in an article you found pertinent.

Often the research in peer-reviewed journals will focus very specifically on children's thinking about a particular aspect of mathematics or a particular teaching strategy and you will be able to use this research to reflect and improve upon your own existing pedagogical subject knowledge.

Government-funded research

In addition to research journals, you should also use government-funded research. When you are reading to specifically learn more about mathematics teaching, you may find government-funded research more accessible, readable and directly related to teaching. Government-funded research often signals the future direction of policy or guidance which keeps you up to date in your professional development.

Below are a number of government-funded publications related to mathematics.

Williams Review

In 2007 the Secretary of State asked Sir Peter Williams to undertake a review of mathematics teaching in early years settings and primary schools. The final report was published a year later drawing on evidence from *robust published research; relevant data and statistics; and a programme of visits to schools and settings throughout England* (Williams, 2008, page 1). It covered a lot of ground, including initial teacher training, continuing professional development, the early years, under-attainment and intervention (specifically the *Every Child Counts* intervention programme), curriculum and pedagogy, and parents and families.

Mathematics specialist teachers (MaST)

Almost immediately some of the recommendations in the report were set in motion by the Labour government, such as the training of Mathematics Specialist Teachers (MaST). The role of the MaST is to champion mathematics in the school, develop their own and their colleagues' mathematics subject and pedagogical knowledge and to be actively involved in mathematics school improvement.

MaST teachers are engaged over a two-year period on a Masters'-level programme worth 60 credits (one-third of an MA). More information can be found at **www.teachernet.gov.uk/ professionaldevelopment/careers/mstp/**.

Developing mathematics in initial teacher training

Another development from the Williams Review was the e-learning resource *Developing mathematics in initial teacher training (DMITT)* (National Strategies, 2010). This resource identified five key priorities for mathematics teaching in the Williams Review. These were:

- guided group work in mathematics;
- high quality mathematical talk;
- oral and mental mathematics;
- using and applying mathematics;
- planning for pupil progression (including transitions).

In addition to these, there is a clear focus on developing mathematical subject and pedagogical knowledge.

Activity

If you have not already done so, familiarise yourself with DMITT online at **http:// nationalstrategies.standards.dcsf.gov.uk/node/461886**. It is accessible to everyone, although you will be required to set up a username and password. Work through the tasks to challenge your own understanding of the key aspects of teaching mathematics listed above.

Ofsted reports

Ofsted funds and produces a number of research reports and surveys related to mathematics. These are often commissioned by the Government to inform policy-making decisions related to curriculum design or pedagogy. This section discusses three research sources produced by Ofsted: the annual report, *Understanding the score*, and *Finnish pupils' success in mathematics*. It is possible to find the most recent research from Ofsted at their website, **www.ofsted.gov.uk**.

Mathematics: Understanding the score

Mathematics: Understanding the score (Ofsted, 2008) is an analysis with detailed evidence from mathematics teaching inspection evidence between 2005 and 2007 from 192 maintained primary and secondary schools in England. The report was presented in two parts, where the first focused on the rising standards in national testing over the last decade (for further discussion on this issue, see Chapter 7). The second part discussed the issues underlying the rises and identified what it refers to as *essential components of effective mathematics teaching* (Ofsted, 2008, page 1).

One year later, this 74-page report was distilled into a booklet *Mathematics: Understanding the score. Improving practice in mathematics teaching at primary level* (Ofsted, 2009). It was sent to primary schools, to help them to put into practice some of the research findings. Crucially, it identified how *it is of vital importance for pupils of all abilities to shift teaching and learning in mathematics away from a narrow emphasis on disparate skills towards a focus on pupils' mathematical understanding* (Ofsted, 2009, page 3). This raises the issue of how teachers can deal with the theory/practice gap (Broekkamp and van Hout-Wolters, 2007; Gert, 2007) to achieve the aspiration set in the booklet. The booklet essentially addresses this by publishing the features of 'good' and 'satisfactory' mathematics teaching with illustrations of the prime and weaker aspects of teaching mathematics in primary schools.

Listed in Table 8.1 are only a few of the features identified in the booklet. These relate to the use of mathematics across the curriculum, and specifically to conceptualising mathematics as reasoning, problem-solving and communication (see Chapter 1 for further discussion), which form the focus of this book.

Activity

As you read the features, consider how important both mathematics subject knowledge and mathematics pedagogical knowledge are in order to demonstrate the aspects of good mathematics teaching. Reflect on how the features of satisfactory mathematics teaching are more routinised and do not utilise as much skill in mathematical subject and pedagogical knowledge.

Features of good mathematics teaching	Features of satisfactory mathematics teaching
The lesson forms a clear part of a developmental sequence and pupils recognise links with earlier work, different parts of mathematics or contexts for its use.	The lesson stands alone adequately but links are superficial; for example, links are made with the previous lesson but not in a way that all the pupils understand.
Non-routine problems, open-ended tasks and investigations are used often by **all** pupils to develop the broader mathematical skills of problem-solving, reasoning and generalising.	Typical lessons consist of routine exercises that develop skills and techniques adequately but pupils have few opportunities to develop reasoning, problem-solving and investigatory skills, or only the higher attainers are given such opportunities.
Pupils develop independence and confidence by recognising when their solutions are correct and persevering to overcome difficulties because they expect to be able to solve problems; the teacher's interventions support them in estimating and checking for themselves.	Support generally offered to pupils does not develop independence in solving complete problems; for example, answers are given too readily or the problem is broken down so much that pupils do not know why the sequence of steps was chosen. Pupils may ask for help at each step and are given directed steps to take rather than interventions that encourage thinking and confidence that they can succeed.
Good use of subject knowledge to capitalise on opportunities to extend understanding, such as through links to other subjects, more complex situations or previously learned mathematics.	Any small slips or vagueness in use of subject knowledge do not prevent pupils from making progress.
Pupils exude enjoyment and involvement in the lesson. Pupils are confident enough to offer right and wrong comments. Pupils naturally listen to and respond to each other's comments, showing engagement with them.	Pupils enjoy making progress in an ordered environment. Some pupils offer responses to whole-class questions. Pupils listen to the teacher's and pupils' contributions and respond to them when asked to.

Table 8.1 Selected features of mathematics teaching from Ofsted (2009)

If you are researching about cross-curricular mathematics, the impact of good subject knowledge in teaching mathematics, aspects of using and applying mathematics, or indeed many other topics, you could use both the report and the primary schools booklet to support your assignment. You may also wish to consider how the findings and recommendations from this research can feed into your target-setting for your professional profile.

Annual report of Her Majesty's Chief Inspector

Every year Ofsted produces a report of Her Majesty's Chief Inspector. This annual report draws on evidence from inspection and regulation across the sectors for which it is responsible (including early years and primary). It is an important document to be aware of because it is presented to Parliament and contains matters that Ofsted considers to be of national importance and interest. Often the content signals changes for education and if you are aware of these elements at 'top level' you will be better prepared to respond as a teacher and trainee teacher.

In the 2009/10 annual report Ofsted (2010) identified the move primary schools are making towards more flexibility in their curriculum. The report states that this move provides opportunities for children to use and apply mathematics across the curriculum. However, it also found that although children find cross-curricular activities *interesting, this cross-curriculum approach to developing numeracy can lack coherence when poorly planned* (para 94).

Activity

Read paragraph 471 from the 2009/10 Ofsted Annual Report, reproduced below. Highlight the key aspects that Ofsted identified are found 'most wanting' in schools causing concern. You may wish to think about your own knowledge and understanding of those aspects in relation to mathematics, using the table below. Two examples are provided for you. Reflect on how you have used this research to impact on your own mathematics teaching.

471. The main issues are similar in primary schools, where standards in writing and mathematics are most often found wanting, followed by English and science. Teachers are often not sufficiently knowledgeable about the levels at which pupils are working and achieving, or practised in matching work to their abilities and using varied methods to promote learning. Their expectations of what pupils could achieve are often too low. Specific weaknesses may be identified, such as in the Early Years Foundation Stage, progress in Key Stage 2, opportunities for outdoor learning, assessment and marking of work, strategies for tackling weaknesses and helping those who find learning a challenge.

Aspect	Level of knowledge and understanding	Actions to take to improve
Pupil levels	Low	Review notes from workshop on levelling children's work; Talk to class teacher about children's levels before starting to plan; Sample children's books; Look at APP grids
Matching work to pupils' abilities	Medium	Familiarise self with workbooks used in school before start of placement; Build up bank of open-ended investigations; Talk to Mathematics Specialist Teacher (MaST teacher) in the school

Research Focus: Finnish pupils' success in mathematics

In September 2010 Ofsted published a report that focused on the factors that contribute positively to Finnish pupils' success in mathematics and considered the implications for policy and practice in England.

This research was undertaken after international comparisons had highlighted Finnish children's success in mathematics as very high. Finland also showed a much narrower gap between the higher and lower attainers compared to England and many other countries. Due to the stability in the country's curriculum, the success is more easily traced over time.

The report identified six key factors that contribute to the Finnish success. These are as follows.

1. The **ethos** in the education system means children's needs are identified quickly and are immediately followed up to enable children to overcome difficulties with their peers.

2. Children learn to **problem-solve** from the outset in realistic or meaningful contexts (this is aided by their high levels of literacy).

3. Textbooks that use problem-solving, thinking and rigour in **applying** mathematical techniques are used to underpin all mathematics work.

4. Teachers ensure that **all children** can carry out the methods needed in each topic.

5. Initial teacher education develops **reflective teachers**, which leads to effective links between theory and practice. Placements have depth and quality, and are shorter than English placements.

6. Teachers are confident in their **subject knowledge** and **pedagogical knowledge** of mathematics and therefore convey confidence in their own and their children's ability to learn mathematics.

Activity

What links can you see between the three Ofsted publications discussed above? You may wish to reflect on your own knowledge, understanding and skills related to these aspects of mathematics education, and if necessary log them in your target-setting document for further developments.

In conclusion to this section on the literature review, your tutors will help you to choose appropriate reading throughout your course, through directed and suggested text. Reading the primary source (that is, the original journal article and not another person's interpretation) will enable you to critique the findings more effectively for your own assignments. However, if you are struggling to find appropriate research articles to read, or if you are struggling to understand them, you will be able to seek help from your library or student support system to help you in your assignments.

The data-handling cycle

In the overview of the improving teaching and learning process we asked you to recall the 'plan, do, review' cycle from Chapter 5. This section clarifies the cycle, in what we call the data handling cycle.

Research Focus: Action research

Zuber-Skerritt (1996) also noticed this three-part cycle when she reviewed a number of action research methodologies. She identified that many of them involved a cyclical process involving: (1) strategic planning, (2) implementation, (3) observation, evaluation and self-evaluation. Do you see a similarity with the three-step data-handling process discussed in Chapter 5?

Plan and do

When you are planning the next steps in the improving teaching and learning process you will think about aspects such as whether you will be using quantitative, qualitative or mixed methods, and whether your data will come from a primary or secondary source. The key question for you should be, 'how am I best going to respond to the question, issue or title I have?'

Next, you have to consider the timescales that you are working in, and realistically how long you will have to carry out what needs to be done to address your question, focus or title. Additionally consider if there are any other constraints that you also have, such as the physical space available to you, other placement expectations or the method of collection you prefer.

We suggest that you try and make your data collection and its method part of what you normally do. This will help you to see the improving teaching and learning process as a natural extension of your professional development, rather than as a bolt-on to your teaching. It also helps you to make the most efficient use of your time in school. Of course this may not be possible and you may have to withdraw children in order to undertake your data collection.

The following case study illustrates how two trainee teachers worked collaboratively to improve their own mathematical pedagogical subject knowledge as well as improving the children's learning in mathematics lessons.

Case Study: Data collection with a teaching partner

Tara: We had this maths assignment where we had to choose an issue that arose from the Williams Review and look at how we could improve our teaching as a result of reading more about it.

Luke: We decided that it would make sense for us to focus on the same thing because we were in the class together. Also, our teacher had just been on a course about high-quality talk in the classroom and so she had just begun to look at that in maths.

Tara: I started and focused on open-ended questioning, particularly looking at getting children to explain their thinking a lot more. I kept to this in my guided group work time during lessons. The teacher was really great because she released Luke from a week's worth of lessons in order to observe me and make notes like you can see here (see Figure 8.2).

Luke: Yeah, I have to admit that at first I wasn't keen to not have my own group in the lesson, but Jackie, our teacher, said that I'd learn just as much if not more by observing someone else in a focused way. She was right.

Interviewer: How did you learn more?

Luke: Well each day Tara and I got together and discussed what I'd observed alongside how she thought it went. The prompt sheet (Figure 8.2) really helped. At first I do admit I thought it was a bit of a pain but I just went along with it. But that discussion was really interesting and the sheet helped to prompt the discussion. I really got into the swing of it and there was loads I'd have forgotten if I hadn't written it down. It was a mess but it doesn't matter. At first, Tara was quite nervous and so she asked the questions quickly and didn't give the children a lot of time to talk or think and she answered the questions for the children! [*Laughs*] I recognised that it was something I was doing too, but I wouldn't have picked up on that if I had just kept doing it.

Tara: I hadn't realised either. I chose the questioning angle for the assignment because I thought it was something I was already good at. By the end of the week I was a lot calmer and that meant the children had more time to think and that gave me more time to be considered in what I said, rather than just say something for the sake of it because I didn't like awkward silences.

$\rightarrow$

Luke: I also liked that I could observe the children. I didn't have to perform so I had the time to do that. And part of the discussion we had afterwards was about which children talked and for how long. That helped me to formulate the focus for my assignment, which was how to encourage the children to talk to each other and learn from each other, rather than having the focus on the teacher more often than not.

Tara: We swapped over the next week and like Luke said, observing someone else in action helps you to learn more than if you're in the thick of it yourself. Luke's focus was a natural extension of my work because he looked at how he could encourage the children to talk to each other, rather than the focus being the teacher and that was great because as Jackie pointed out, we're all here for the children and they got so much out of us having to do our assignment.

Observation schedule for Luke

Day: Wed 23rd.

Time start	Time end	Who	What	Other
10:23	10:25	Tara	Recap on main part of lesson.	
10:25	10:25	Tara	Q - What know about fractions	Shelly looking off into space
10:25	10:27	Simon Kelley Poppy	S - ½ · drawn ○ K - two half = Whole. P - 'Fourths' - 'Quarter'	Good prompt to Poppy - What do you mean?
10:27	10:27	Tara	Brought Shelly back with Q-what do you know?	
10:27		Shelly	Nothing.	
	10.28	Tara	Have a think	You wouldn't have done this on Mon!!
			Talk to person next to you.	Could they have recorded ideas?
10.32	10.32	Tara to Shelly	Q-Is there something you'd like to tell us about fractions?	
10.32		Shelly	¼ larger than ¼ & ¼ > 1/10	Result!

Figure 8.2 Observation schedule

In the case study we can see how Tara and Luke were both systematic in the way they collected their data and then discussed it. They used logical thinking to identify cause and effect within each lesson as well as the next steps they could take in improving their teaching and the children's learning.

There are many methods of data collection, including surveys, questionnaires, tests, observation, document analysis, literature reviews, and case studies. It is important you understand what these are so that you are able to select which type of data are best to collect for your purposes, and to analyse effectively the data you have collected. You use your mathematical skills in reasoning, communication and problem-solving to plan and carry out the methodology and methods you used. For example, you are required to discuss why you chose a particular method, making connections with views from the literature and your own experience.

Review

After all your planning and data collection have been carried out, you will need to review your data in order to generate findings. Part of this element will be deciding how to make your data more manageable, by collating and representing them effectively. The following case study shows how one trainee teacher, Sinead, was not sure how to review her data once she had collected them.

Case Study: Analysing data and presenting findings

Sinead had collected in the survey responses from the parents in the two Year 3 classes where she was on placement. The survey, looking at parents' opinions of cross-curricular mathematics, produced the following data from Question 3: 'I believe children at primary school should be taught maths basics before being expected to use maths in other contexts.'

Category	No. of responses	Percentage
Strongly agree (5)	4	8
Agree (4)	21	44
Unsure/neutral (3)	9	19
Disagree (2)	11	23
Strongly disagree (1)	3	6
Total:	48	100

Once Sinead had the data, she was not sure how to analyse them in order to gain more clarity around her findings. She asked one of her friends, who suggested that she find the mean of the data.

This gave an answer of 3, which she calculated using:

$$\frac{(4 \times 5)+(21 \times 4)+(9 \times 3)+(11 \times 2)+(3 \times 1)}{48}$$

She didn't find this particularly helpful because she thought that the mean (3.25) identified the category 'unsure/neutral', and if she was to use this finding, it would imply that overall, the parents had no opinion about the issue. However, intuitively, she knew that this was not the case. After all, 52 per cent of parents agreed or strongly agreed. When she talked it over with her tutor, the tutor explained that she was treating the numbers 1–5 associated with the Likert Scale categories as an amount rather than a category. In this situation it wasn't realistic to use the mean of 3.25 to present the findings, because although the categories were labelled with whole numbers, those numbers did not represent a numerical value and therefore 3.25 had no real meaning.

→

Instead, they ordered the data and found the midpoint (the median), which was 4.

5, 5, 5, 5, 4, 4, 4, 4, 4, 4, 4, 4, 4, 4, 4, 4, 4, 4, 4, 4, 4, 4, 4, 4, 3, 3, 3, 3, 3, 3, 3, 3, 3, 2, 2, 2, 2, 2, 2, 2, 2, 2, 2, 2, 1, 1, 1

Sinead explained to her tutor that that was more helpful, because the median identified a category (agree) with which to present and then discuss the findings of her research. To read more about the purpose of number, read Chapter 2.

However you decide to collate and represent the data, constantly check that your decisions are supporting you to inform your question, issue or title.

How you collate your data will depend on the type of data you have. If they are quantitative, you will represent the numerical data in tables and charts. Qualitative data require different treatment during review, but it is important to remember that qualitative data can also be represented in a numerical way. See Further Reading for where to go if you need help in collating, representing and reviewing quantitative or qualitative data. Below is an activity involving an example of how a trainee teacher interpreted her findings.

Activity

Think about this trainee teacher's statement, taken from a mathematics education assignment. What do you think are the strengths and weaknesses of the discussion?

Discussion

My findings identified that 50% of all teachers found that the introduction of the whole class teaching element of the NNS had no impact on the way that they taught maths (see Table 1). This supports the findings of Smith et al (2004) who show that more traditional ways of teaching the whole class have not been dramatically changed. They state, 'our findings suggest new "top-down" curriculum initiatives like the NLS and NNS, while bringing about a scenario of change in curriculum design, often leave deeper levels of pedagogy untouched. Traditional patterns of whole class interaction persist, with teacher questioning only rarely being used to assist pupils to articulate more complete or elaborated ideas as recommended by the strategies' (p.409).

Now have a look at Table 1 that is referred to. What do you think, now?

Teacher	Did the NNS have an impact on the way you taught the whole class?	
	YES	NO
M	✓	
S	✓	
F		✓
J		✓

Now have a look at an excerpt from the trainee's methodology section. Any further thoughts?

I used a semi-structured interview because it allowed me to use 'prompts and probes' (Cohen, Manion and Morrison, 2007, p. 361). I thought that these would be useful for me to 'extend, elaborate, add to, provide detail for, clarify or qualify their response' (ibid.). I interviewed the four teachers with whom I had most contact. These were M, my mentor, S, the Y1 teacher in the parallel class, and F and J who were job-share teachers in my Y1 placement class.

This trainee's work shows that it is very tempting to make generalised comments, but when the type of data you have collected does not lend itself to generalisation this is not appropriate. At first, the trainee's discussion appears very good. She has linked some findings to a research article she has read and explains how her findings resonate with the literature. However, when the data table is examined, it is possible to see that only four teachers were asked the question. Additionally, when delving further into the method she used, we see that the teachers were all from one school. Therefore, the trainee should not generalise to say '50 per cent of teachers'. Instead she could have written '50 per cent of the teachers I interviewed' or better still 'two out of the four teachers I interviewed'.

Systematic review

This element requires you to step back and make decisions to consolidate prior knowledge and clarify what steps are to be taken next in a systematic, logical and reasoned way. In her meta-analysis, Zuber-Skeritt (1996) also identified this element. She referred to it as a critical and self-critical evaluation on the three-part cycle and it is used to inform and make decisions for the next cycle of research. We can see this in the improving teaching and learning process diagram in Figure 8.1 where the systematic review feeds into the dissemination of findings as well as back into the beginnings again.

Crucially, it is the systematic review of the three-part handling data process that makes the assessed academic work you carry out as a trainee teacher stand apart from the other data handling processes you use in your day-to-day work. Cohen *et al.* (2000, page 227) explain how this enables *a self-conscious awareness of the effects that the participants-as-practitioners-and-researchers are having on the research process.*

Gravemeijer and Cobb (2006) refer to the systematic review as a retrospective analysis. They explain how retrospective analysis is context-specific, but it is essential that the outcomes of the retrospective analysis have been systematically developed through all the types of data you have collected.

What have you discovered and what have you learned?

We offer you this simple but effective way of trying to carry out your systematic review. The systematic review provides you the opportunity to consider (a) what you have discovered, and (b) what you have learned.

What you have discovered refers to your findings. Normally you will select the findings that you will discuss later and they will be represented in a form that you used during your earlier review of the data.

What you have learned refers to your discussion. In the discussion you will need to review the extent to which your data are valid and reliable, and to what extent they show any bias. You will need to consider things such as questionnaires and interviews. Were your questions written in a way that only allowed answers that would agree or disagree with your viewpoint? Did you leave out anything that you disagreed with? Your results may well be valid as in the previous case study but taken in context they are not very reliable and could not be used to contribute to a deeper understanding of the issue under discussion. This is also the opportunity you have to draw some conclusions related to the question, issue or title and suggest ways in which this small research study could be developed further.

There are many, many ways in which you can present what you have learned. In his book *Researching your own practice*, Professor of mathematics education John Mason offers 'the discipline of noticing' which he describes as a method that attempts to be *systematic and methodical without being mechanical* that supports practitioners to develop their professional practice (Mason, 2002, page 59).

Research Focus: Account of and accounting for

Mason (2002) distinguishes between an account of and accounting for. Providing an objective account of a situation or event provides your audience with the situation first, before you provide them with your interpretations. It can be likened to explaining a film segment, so that your audience can recognise the actions of the people involved. Once an account of a situation has been given, it is then possible to account for the situation by introducing *explanation, theorising and perhaps judgement and evaluation* (Mason, 2002, page 40) of the situation.

By using accounts of and then accounting for, it is possible to support your validation of the situation or events you are analysing in your research.

If you are new to the improving teaching and learning process, you may think that this is the point at which your question, issue or title is answered or adequately addressed. However, one exciting (and often also challenging) component of this process is that if you have undertaken your research effectively, you are likely to have raised a lot more questions than you have answered. You may recall this was identified as the 'knowledge gap' in Molinero and García-

Madruga's (2010) research, introduced in Chapter 5. You will see in Figure 8.1 how the process can feed from the systematic review back into the beginning.

Dissemination of findings

No matter how you are required to disseminate your work, the purpose is three-fold.

1. Your experience during the improving teaching and learning process can be assessed.

2. Your findings are shared more widely.

3. To receive feedback from your tutors, and/or colleagues.

It is likely that point 1 is the main reason that you complete the piece for submission. However, the other two points are also important. No matter how your work is published, you are responsible for sharing your findings with others. At the very least, your marking tutors will read your work and most will tell you that they continue to learn from reading students' assignments. If your publication is a poster, podcast, presentation or journal article you are probably sharing this with a wider audience and you will become a peer tutor and also receive feedback from your colleagues. This leads us to the final point. We would encourage you to think of your 'product' as a critical component of the improving teaching and learning process. By receiving feedback from your tutor, peers or teaching colleagues (depending on the method/s of assessment), your systematic review can continue. In turn, this may lead you into exploring the issue or topic further, either within your ITT course or deeper research beyond your course. This is how your research in higher education may lead you into Masters' and doctoral-level research in the future.

Learning Outcomes Review

This chapter has presented the improving teaching and learning process, which is integral to your ITT assignments and therefore your professional development. It has outlined some of the mathematical skills, knowledge and understanding that you will be using and applying as you follow the process. One element of the process is the literature review. This chapter has introduced several mathematics education peer-reviewed and professional journals. It has discussed recent, relevant government-funded research publications. The improving teaching and learning process enables you to teach all subjects of the curriculum including mathematics.

Self-assessment questions
1. What does research undertaken by Ofsted tell us about cross-curricular mathematics teaching?
2. What are the advantages of thinking about the improving teaching and learning process as an integral component of your professional development, rather than simply thinking of assignments as an additional burden?

---

3. Recreate the improving teaching and learning process. Choose one assignment or research project you have undertaken recently and make notes on your reflections on each element in the process. Which element(s) do you need to learn more about?

4. Explain the difference between peer-reviewed and professional journals.

Further Reading

Cohen, L., Manion, L. and Morrison, K. (2011) *Research methods in education*. London: Routledge. This explores in great depth all the methods of data collection you or your children will use.

Developing mathematics in initial teacher education is an online resource for primary trainees. This material was based on a number of principles outlined in the Williams Report (high-quality mathematical talk, oral and mental mathematics, using and applying mathematics, planning for pupil progression, and guided group work), including the opportunity to develop some aspects of your mathematics subject knowledge. **http:// nationalstrategies.standards.dcsf.gov.uk/node/461819**

Mason, J. (2002) *Researching your own practice: The discipline of noticing*. London: Routledge. This explains noticing as a discipline for developing your professional practice. Chapter 3 introduces account of and accounting for as presented in the research focus presented in this chapter.

Miles, M.B. and Huberman, M. (1994) *Qualitative data analysis*. Thousand Oaks, CA: Sage Publications and Strauss, A.C. and Corbin, J.M. (1998) *Basics of qualitative research: Techniques and procedures for developing grounded theory*. Thousand Oaks, CA: Sage Publications both support you in analysing qualitative data.

Mooney, C., Hansen, A., Wrathmell, R., Fox, S. and Ferrie, L. (2011) Handling data and probability. This is Chapter 6 in Mooney, C. *et al. Primary mathematics: Knowledge and understanding*. Exeter: Learning Matters. It explains the difference between continuous and discrete data.

Williams, P. (2008) *Independent Review of Mathematics Teaching in Early Years Settings and Primary Schools. Final Report*. London: DCSF. Google DCSF-00433-2008 to find an online copy of this important report. **http://www.education.gov.uk/publications/standard/ publicationdetail/page1/DCSF-00433-2008**

References

Biesta, G. (2007) Bridging the gap between educational research and educational practice: The need for critical distance. *Educational Research and Evaluation*, 13 (13): 295–301.

Broekkamp, H. and van Hout-Wolters, B. (2007) The gap between educational research and practice: A literature review, symposium and questionnaire. *Educational Research and Evaluation,* 13 (13): 203–220.

Cobb, P., Confrey, I., diSessa, A., Lehrer, R. and Schauble, L. (2003) Design experiments in educational research. *Educational Researcher,* 32 (4): 9–13.

Cohen, L., Manion, L. and Morrison, K. (2000) *Research methods in education* (5th edition). London: RoutledgeFalmer.

Cohen, L., Manion, L. and Morrison, K. (2007) *Research methods in education* (6th edition). Abingdon: Routledge.

Gravemeijer, K. and Cobb, P. (2006) Design research from a learning design perspective, in van den Akker, J., Gravemeijer, K., McKenney, S. and Nieveen, N. (eds) *Educational design research.* London: Routledge, 17–51.

Lee, H. (2005) Understanding and assessing preservice teachers' reflective thinking. *Teaching and Teacher Education,* 21 (6): 699–715.

Oates, T. (2010) *Could do better: Using international comparisons to refine the national curriculum in England.* Cambridge Assessment. Available at **www.cambridgeassessment. org.uk/ca/digitalAssets/188853_Could_do_better_ FINAL_inc_foreword.pdf** (accessed 27/01/11).

Ofsted (2008) Mathematics: Understanding the score. London: Ofsted. Available at **www.ofsted.gov.uk/Ofsted-home/Publications-and-research/Browse-all-by/Documents-by-type/Thematic-reports/Mathematics-understanding-the-score** (accessed 27/01/11).

Ofsted (2009) *Mathematics: Understanding the score. Improving practice in mathematics teaching at primary level.* London: Ofsted. Available at **www.ofsted.gov.uk/Ofsted-home/Publications-and-research/Browse-all-by/Documents-by-type/Thematic-reports/Mathematics-understanding-the-score-Improving-practice-in-mathematics-primary** (accessed 27/01/11).

Ofsted (2010) *The annual report of Her Majesty's Chief Inspector of Education, Children's Services and Skills 2009/10.* London: TSO. Available at **www.ofsted.gov.uk/Ofsted-home/Publications-and-research/Browse-all-by/Annual-Report/2009-10/The-Annual-Report-of-Her-Majesty-s-Chief-Inspector-of-Education-Children-s-Services-and-Skills-2009-10** (accessed 27/01/11).

Williams, P. (2008) *Independent review of mathematics teaching in early years settings and primary schools. Final report.* London: DCSF.

Zuber-Skerrit, O. (1996) Emancipatory action research for organisational change and management development, in Zuber-Skerrit, O. (ed.) *New directions in action research.* London: Falmer.

Model answers

Chapter 1

1. Why do you think mathematics is often taught as a discrete lesson and not integrated as other subjects might more easily be?

Mathematics is often seen as a discrete subject. Many teachers (see the Williams Review, 2008) do not necessarily see how mathematics is integral to many subjects and how other subjects can also develop children's mathematical skills.

2. Identify five mathematical skills, knowledge or understanding you have used and applied in the last 24 hours.

Answers will vary.

3. Why does Ma1: Using and applying mathematics not have its own discrete programme of study (PoS) with objectives listed as the other PoS do?

In the 1988 National Curriculum, Ma1 was listed separately. In an attempt to reflect that Using and applying is interwoven throughout all the PoS, Ma1 was embedded at the beginning of each PoS in the 1999 National Curriculum.

4. What are the three skills in Ma1: Using and applying mathematics?

The three skills are reasoning, problem-solving, and communication.

5. What key skills and thinking skills in the National Curriculum (pages 20–22) can you associate with Using and applying mathematics?

It is no doubt possible to make links with all the key skills. However, most pertinent are communication, application of number, and problem-solving. All the thinking skills should be included: information processing, reasoning, enquiry, creative thinking and evaluation.

6. What subject(s) do not relate to mathematics or use mathematical skills in any way?

We hope you realised that this was a trick question! As you read this book, you will see that we have provided at least one example from every National Curriculum subject about how mathematics relates to all areas of the curriculum.

Chapter 2

1. How might providing the answer to a group of children, rather than a set of closed questions, encourage their use and application of number?

Giving all children the opportunity to think about the 'answer' enables them to think mathematically in a creative way. It also provides you with an opportunity to assess their knowledge and understanding.

2. What are the benefits of using the outdoors as a learning environment?

According to Lin (2002), mathematics trails provide the opportunity to practise thinking, provide a supplementary teaching resource for teachers, consolidate knowledge and skills, connect life-school contexts and develop communication skills. You may have identified further benefits.

3. Identify a link between poetry and music.

One link you may have identified is the use of rhythm in the prose. Another might be the form of the piece, such as ABA or AABBA.

4. How might you use photographs of post boxes to explore history, in a similar way to the coins in the case study in this chapter?

The date of production of all post boxes is revealed in the royal insignia that can be found on them. Photos can be ordered chronologically. This task can also be enhanced with the use of postmarked stamps.

Chapter 3

1. Continue to make a bank of words that are ambiguous. Include the mathematical and everyday definitions.

Answers may vary. See definitions of volume, capacity, weight and mass in Chapter 4.

2. Create an inclusive definition of a square using its symmetry properties

A square has order of rotation of four. It also has four lines of symmetry.

3. Define *congruent* and *similar*.

Congruent means exactly the same. Similar means identical shape, just a different size.

4. Define *area* and *perimeter*

The perimeter is the length of the sides encompassing an area. It comes from the Greek *peri* meaning 'around' and *meter* meaning 'measure'. The area is the space that is encompassed by the perimeter.

Chapter 4

1. How many units of time can you identify?

The following table shows units of time, from longest to shortest.

Unit	Size
Exasecond, used when referring to the age of the universe	10^{18} s
Millennium	1000 years
Century	100 years
Indiction, European historical cycle for dating medieval documents	15 years
Decade	10 years
Lustrum, the period between Ancient Rome census taking	5 years
Olympiad, the four-year period from 1 January of the year a summer Olympics is taking place	4 years
Gregorian year	Approximately 365 days
Leap year	Approximately 366 days
Year	12 months
Quarter	3 months
Month	28–31 days
Fortnight	2 weeks
Week	7 days
Day	24 hours
Hour	60 minutes
Minute	60 seconds
Second	1 second (SI base unit)
Millisecond	One thousandth of a second, or 0.001 s or 10^{-3} s
Microsecond	10^{-6} s
Nanosecond, the time it takes for molecules to fluoresce	10^{-9} s
Picosecond	10^{-12} s
Femtosecond	10^{-15} s
Attosecond, currently the shortest time that humankind can measure	10^{-18} s

2. If you speak another language, think about how the number system is expressed in that language. What are the similarities and differences to English? If you do not speak another language then use the internet to help you to do this.

While the answer will depend on the language you chose, think about how the teen numbers and tens numbers are expressed, and how numbers with three digits are structured. For example, some languages will have new names for the teen numbers (e.g. 15 in Spanish is *quince*) and others will generate the teen numbers by bringing together ten and the unit (e.g. in New Zealand Maori, 15 is ten and five: *tekau ma rima*). **www.zompist.com/numbers.htm**

provides the numbers 1–10 in over five thousand languages! Searching for '100 squares in different languages' will help you and children make further sense of other countries' number systems.

3. What does the term *conservation* mean?

Conservation is a term coined by Piaget. It refers to a child's ability to be able to reason that two quantities are the same or not. Piaget identified that if a child is working in the pre-operational stage, they will not be able conserve amounts. Later research has shown that it is not necessarily the readiness of a child to be able to understand conservation, but the context and way in which the conservation task is carried out.

Chapter 5

1. The introduction of this chapter asked you to keep Articles 12 and 14 from the United Nations Convention on the Rights of the Child (UNCRC) in your mind as you read this chapter. How do you think the knowledge, skills and understanding that are developed through handling data empower children to enact this right?

Handling data is a tool that enables children to carry out the rights the UNCRC gives them. This is because handling data provides an opportunity for children to express themselves, and be able to *seek, receive and impart information and ideas of all kinds, regardless of frontiers, either orally, in writing or in print, in the form of art, or through any other media of the child's choice.*

2. Why is the data-handling process seen as a cycle, rather than as a linear process?

Part of the data-handling process is reviewing. It is during the reviewing process that further questions may be asked, or that gaps in the findings may be identified. Seeing the process as a cycle means that these questions or gaps can be addressed.

3. Using ICT can empower children to analyse data. Make a list of the affordances that ICT offers over manipulating data by hand.

ICT affords the user a number of advantages over manipulating data by hand. For example, once data are entered a graph can be created, often at the touch of a button. Data can be changed, or new graphs can be created, very quickly indeed. This means that more time can be spent on analysing the data and presenting the data most effectively, rather than tediously manipulating the data by hand. Research has shown how using computer-generated graphs enables children to explore complex data meaningfully. Using spreadsheets allows children to order data, find the sum or the mean quickly. Amending the data automatically updates the sum or mean if formulas are used. When presenting findings using ICT, the text, tables and graphs can be moved around quickly and easily in order for the children to present the most polished piece, in order to communicate with the audience. Using ICT (email, blogs, school website) also enables children to communicate their findings with a wider audience. This is not an exhaustive list and you may have identified other affordances of ICT.

Chapter 6

1. The curriculum subjects that are required to be taught cannot fit into a school year if they are taught separately. How can teachers effectively meet the requirements of the National Curriculum, given that this is the case?

One pragmatic response to addressing this issue is to approach learning and planning in an integrated, cross-curricular way. This has a positive effect on children's learning because the artificial barriers that have been created between the subjects in the National Curriculum are broken down.

2. Provide at least five reasons for integrating out-of-school visits into your learning provision.

Your list may have included the following reasons (taken from Coughlin, 2010). Provide a lived learning experience, connecting with first-hand experience; link children's learning to a particular place, person or object; increase collaboration between children and teachers; can be inexpensive; can help children to explore 'powerful ideas' (such as 'change'); hands-on activities enable children to recall information; offer high-quality learning resources. You may be able to identify more ideas.

3. List some of the strategies that you have seen teachers using to ensure that class resources are not wasted.

Answers will vary. Some may include: handing out the required number of resources to the children; encouraging children to turn a page over if they want to start again; locked resource cupboard where children may not enter; password-protected photocopy machines; limit of printer cartridges; bulk buying; encouraging children to bring in things from home.

Chapter 7

1. Use a diagram to show the relationship between the following stakeholders, to map the reporting processes in school: headteacher, school management team, parent, governors, child, teacher, school improvement partner (SIP) from the local authority, Department for Education

Your diagram may look something like this:

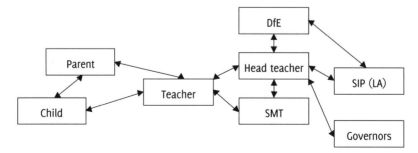

2. Name as many different types of assessment as you can.

Formative, summative, ipsative, assessment for learning, assessment of learning, diagnostic, objective, subjective, formal, informal, internal, external.

3. Identify similarities between the use of APP to assess children's learning and the way in which you are assessed against the standards for QTS.

Some of the similarities you may have identified might be:

- progress is tracked;
- a range of evidence is used;
- focused areas for development are identified and individual targets are agreed;
- both are a form of assessment for learning;
- the materials are used as a basis for further reflection and discussion, reflecting a collaborative approach to learning.

Chapter 8

1. What does research undertaken by Ofsted tell us about cross-curricular mathematics teaching?

Each of the Ofsted documents discussed in this chapter identifies the need for a move away from *a narrow emphasis on disparate skills towards a focus on children's mathematical understanding* (Ofsted, 2009, page 3). The 2009/10 annual report states that although children enjoy cross-curricular mathematics, it warns of the potential lack of coherence when planning is poor. *Finnish pupils' success in mathematics* explains how in Finland children learn to solve problems from a young age, using realistic or meaningful contexts. Problem-solving, thinking and rigour in applying mathematical techniques underpin all mathematics work.

Understanding the score. Improving practice in mathematics teaching at primary level (Ofsted, 2009) identifies the following features of good teaching.

- Non-routine problems, open-ended tasks and investigations are used often by all pupils to develop the broader mathematical skills of problem-solving, reasoning and generalising.
- Pupils develop independence and confidence by recognising when their solutions are correct and persevering to overcome difficulties because they expect to be able to solve problems; the teacher's interventions support them in estimating and checking for themselves.
- Good use of subject knowledge is made to capitalise on opportunities to extend understanding, such as through links to other subjects, more complex situations or previously learned mathematics.
- Pupils exude enjoyment and involvement in the lesson. Pupils are confident enough to offer right and wrong comments. Pupils naturally listen to and respond to each other's comments, showing engagement with them.

2. What are the advantages of thinking about the improving teaching and learning process as an integral component of your professional development, rather than simply thinking of assignments as an additional burden?

As you complete your ITT assignments you will follow the improving teaching and learning process. Your assignments are designed to develop your teaching and therefore the children's learning throughout your course. If you keep this in mind, you will see the process as a whole and this will help you to see it as a valuable part of your training rather than a series of disjointed hoops that you are required to jump through.

3. Recreate the improving teaching and learning process. Choose one assignment or research project you have undertaken recently and make notes on your reflections on each element in the process. Which element(s) do you need to learn more about?

Answers will vary.

4. Explain the difference between peer-reviewed and professional journals.

A peer-reviewed journal is one in which articles that are submitted for approval are sent anonymously to other experts in the field. They are only published once they have been checked for accuracy and reliability, and any necessary revisions made. Peer-reviewed journals stipulate the process for submitting, explaining how the peer reviewing happens. Non-peer-reviewed journals, or professional journals, are not as strictly reviewed.

Index

Added to a page number 'f' denotes a figure and 't' denotes a table.